Coaching with Empathy

Coaching in Practice series

The aim of this series is to help coaching professionals gain a broader understanding of the challenges and issues they face in coaching, enabling them to make the leap from being a 'good-enough' coach to an outstanding one. This series is an essential aid for both the novice coach eager to learn how to grow a coaching practice, and the more experienced coach looking for new knowledge and strategies. Combining theory with practice, the series provides a comprehensive guide to becoming successful in this rapidly expanding profession.

Published and forthcoming titles:

Coaching with Empathy

Anne Brockbank and Ian McGill

Mc Graw Hill Education Open University Press

Open University Press
McGraw-Hill Education
McGraw-Hill House
Shoppenhangers Road
Maidenhead
Berkshire
England
SL6 2QL

email: enquiries@openup.co.uk
world wide web: www.openup.co.uk

and Two Penn Plaza, New York, NY 10121-2289, USA

First published 2013

A catalogue record of this book is available from the British Library

ISBN-13: 978-0-33-524655-7 (pb)
ISBN-10: 0-335-24655-9
e-ISBN: 978-0-33-524656-4

Library of Congress Cataloging-in-Publication Data
CIP data applied for

Typeset by Aptara, Inc.

Fictitious names of companies, products, people, characters and/or data that may be used
herein (in case studies or in examples) are not intended to
represent any real individual, company, product or event.

For our grandchildren

Contents

Series Editor's Foreword

For many years in coaching it was often assumed that something called 'business' or 'executive' coaching meant excluding the world of emotion because senior executives were somehow able to bypass all the normal human feelings while they were at work. Coaches and their clients could collude to pretend that this was so, even while the client's distress made it clear that feelings were all too apparent at work, just as they are at home. Fearful of getting into therapeutic territory, lip service was paid to the alleged importance of something labelled 'rapport' or 'empathy', but then the whole apparently messy subject was scurried over as a bit of an embarrassment. If not this, then there was often another assumption that empathy is so obvious a skill that everyone already knows how to do it.

This timely and necessary book is a wonderful corrective. For the first time, we have a detailed explanation of what empathy is, why it matters so much and what can go wrong when it is missing. Equally importantly, there is a wholly original and easily followed guide about how to create and sustain it.

Perhaps it is not by chance that this book is appearing at the same time as neuroscience is showing us that emotion is the dominant part of the human brain, and that we ignore this at our peril, whether as coaches or clients. Everything in coaching is about trust between coach and client, and the only way to create trust is through skilled and sustained empathy. The book also has much sensible and practical guidance on how to avoid getting out of your depth, working within the boundaries of your skill and knowledge.

Anne Brockbank and Ian McGill have many years between them as leading practitioners and teachers in the fields of therapy, mentoring, coaching and action learning. I commend this book to you for its human approach, its many fascinating case studies and the light it will shed on your everyday practice as a coach.

Jenny Rogers
Series Editor

Acknowledgements

As always, we wish to recognize the wealth of wisdom we have gained from our work with our clients. The coaching stories told here (with permission) are composites of many varied coaching relationships. In addition, we wish to thank Helene Donnelly for the DADCC case study; and Ann de Kock and Rose Ricks for their contributions.

We are grateful to Ged O'Connor who provided original material for the illustrations and Tim Walker, Martin Bellman and Ben Cahill who kindly read the text in draft. However we take responsibilty for any errors in the text.

We thank Jenny Rogers for her helpful advice and the Open University team for all their support. We take full responsibility for the finished product and we are happy to receive readers' comments and enquiries.

A.Brockbank@mailbox.ulcc.ac.uk
I.McGill@mailbox.ulcc.ac.uk

www.BrockbankMcGill.co.uk

1 Why use empathy in coaching?

Why are we writing a book about empathy in coaching? Most books on coaching do not even mention empathy. If they do, it is assumed the reader knows what is meant. If empathy is mentioned, readers will search in vain for how to do it. Empathy is central to coaching. Indeed, we assert that without empathy, a coach will limit their effectiveness and the outcomes for their client. In writing this book, we are aiming to remedy a significant gap as well as enable coaches to review their practice and enhance their skills in incorporating empathy into their work.

As coaches and trainers, we use empathy in our own work, finding it valuable for our clients by enabling them to capture their emotional context. In our experience, this helps clients to countenance the possibility of change. We have also received empathy from expert practitioners and benefited from it ourselves.

In this chapter, first of all, we define what empathy is and, more importantly, what it is not. Second, we identify empathy as a key to change, particularly big change in people. Third, we consider why coaching with empathy will benefit clients, teams and organizations.

What is empathy?

People are often puzzled about what empathy is, often confusing it with sympathy or pity. Sympathy means 'feeling sorry for'. Coaches are not expected to feel sorry for their clients, although this may happen sometimes. So if empathy is not sympathy, what is it? To be empathic as a coach, you will need three components:

- what your client is feeling, expressed by your client in words or non-verbal behaviour;
- the experience and/or behaviour which is the source of that feeling, revealed by what your client has already said;
- communication from you as coach to your client of that information in full.

Examples of each of these components are given in the case study below.
To summarize these three components, we define empathy as:

> An understanding of the world from the other's point of view, their feelings, experience and behaviour, and *the communication of that understanding to the other in full.*

The other person here may be a client, colleague, friend or partner, as empathy is an interpersonal skill. However, we will now use a case study to explain how empathy can be used by a coach in an organizational context.

Elizabeth, an independent coach

Elizabeth is listening to her client Eric, a qualified accountant with 15 years' experience, describe his working relationship with his boss, Jason, a senior partner in a global consultancy firm. Eric relates how Jason has apparently ignored his suggestions about the approach he is taking to one of their customers. Eric appears to think he should adopt the approach implicit in Jason's traditional style. Eric has previously shown his desire to fit in with the company in order to become a partner himself in the near future.

While listening, Elizabeth is aware of Eric's increasing pace and volume of speaking, and a slight change in his physical demeanour, revealing his feelings about Jason.

Eric suddenly stops speaking, having come to a pause in his account of Jason's attitude towards him. Elizabeth decides to say:

'Eric, you're angry with Jason because he seems to be ignoring your expertise.'

Eric, now looking directly at Elizabeth, pauses a moment and responds: 'God, I hadn't realized I felt so strongly about it, I mean, Jason. That's it, I am.'

Elizabeth has recognized Eric's feelings which were expressed non-verbally, his stated description of Jason's stance towards him, which appears to be the reason for his feeling, and she has communicated this fully to Eric.

Recognition of what your client is feeling is the first part of empathy. Then the reasons for their feelings in terms of their experience is the second. The response you as coach make, to communicate that understanding to your client, is the third. The three components are necessary for effective empathy and all feature in modern definitions of empathy.

For many people, the idea of empathy is just too 'touchy feely' for the business context, or indeed any context other than therapy. It is true that most of what is known about empathy comes from the world of therapy. However, there is a good reason for this. Empathy is used in therapy to trigger the will to change in a client and this is where it is useful in coaching.

However, coaching is not the same as therapy. Empathy in coaching is used to do the following:

- to support the all-important *relationship* between coach and client;
- to acknowledge the *reasons* behind a client's situation; and
- to calm the client's instinctive *reactions* to threatening change.

The three Rs – relationship, reasons and reactions – are what are important.

Relationship

The most important factor in coaching outcomes is the *relationship* between the coach and their client. The outcome is more influenced by the coaching relationship than the knowledge, qualities, experience, techniques, training, background, or even the age or gender of the coach. The coach and client are not 'in a relationship' in the traditional sense, which is often code for 'having an affair' in today's world. They are collaborating in a professional enterprise for the benefit of the client which the coach is trained to support. Coaches also do not need to be expert in their client's field. What they do need is expertise in creating a relationship with their client, and this is where empathy comes in. How the coach relates to the client is key, not whether the coach knows about the particular field the client works in.

Reasons

For clients, a coach who offers empathy has listened carefully and recognized their situation, exactly as it is experienced by them. This important recognition is what is known as being non-directive as it begins from the client's own experience rather than the coach's. For non-directive coaching, the coach resists the temptation to tell their client what to do or give them advice. As Gore Vidal said: 'All the problems of the world would be solved if only people took my advice.' The reality is that adults rarely act on advice. For many coaches (ourselves included), it may be difficult to resist giving advice. Non-directive coaching is easier if empathy is included.

Response

The neuroscience and psychology of coaching tell us that emotion dominates behaviour, although this is largely denied in modern workplaces. The coach/client relationship provides a safe place where hidden emotional blocks to change may be processed. This does not mean lying on a couch, taking part in New Age techniques, or any other outlandish activities. Empathy in coaching is part of the ordinary spoken exchange between coach and client.

Why does your empathy have to be communicated? Your client may assume that you have fully understood their situation. However, in the absence of any response from you, they may just assume they have not been heard and therefore not understood. The science of coaching reveals that as humans we respond to emotion in others by a matching sense, a mirror image of the other's emotion. This matching sense inside the coach is invisible to their client unless the coach communicates it. Just feeling the same as your client is nice but not enough. For empathy in coaching, it is necessary for you as a coach to communicate what your matching sense is, *by conveying verbally what you have understood your client's feeling to be.*

Used effectively, this is the skill in action known as empathy, and can be described as a day-to-day skill because anyone can do it, as empathy can be learnt quite easily. Lots of people use empathy quite naturally, especially women, who tend to be socialized to be more responsive to feelings. This redresses the balance as men may more easily adopt the skill of assertion, which they are socialized to use more than women. Because empathy may be used unconsciously, it is not always recognized as a valuable and learnable skill.

Empathy as intelligence

Empathy appears as a managerial and leadership skill as part of what is known as emotional intelligence. In the past 20 years emotional intelligence, sometimes called EQ as a way of comparing it with IQ, has been seen as increasingly important to organizational performance. Daniel Goleman's best-selling book, *Emotional Intelligence* (1995) offered an easy way of understanding that business success depended as much on emotional as on intellectual factors. It made a compelling case for saying that the ability to understand and manage yourself and to create rapport with others was an essential precursor to managing others. The messages of the book were radical at the time and in many ways they still are: Do you know the impact you have on others? Can you manage your own feelings of anger and anxiety? Can you easily put yourself in others' shoes? Empathy is among the skills that enable you to take emotion on board with yourself and with others.

This new emphasis in business on emotional intelligence has led to empathy popping up as a quality in person specifications without it being totally understood as a learnable skill. Our suggestion comes from the evidence that empathy can be learnt and can work between people. Simon Baron-Cohen in his book *Zero Degrees of Empathy* (2011: 127) declares that 'Empathy is a universal solvent – any problem immersed in empathy becomes soluble.' Baron-Cohen introduced the idea of rating a person's empathy and provides a method to measure it.

Levels of empathy

In this book we build on the work of Carl Rogers (1951), Gerard Egan (1990), David Mearns and Brian Thorne (1988, 2000), who developed levels of empathy in their work as psychotherapists, trainers and developers. The levels of empathy are important for coaches to understand as different levels are appropriate in different situations. There are four levels of empathy:

- *Zero empathy*: silence, giving advice, making judgements, asking questions, etc.
- *Partial empathy*: responding to one identified feeling out of two or more.
- *Primary empathy*: responding to emotion or feeling based on verbal or non-verbal cues.
- *Advanced empathy*: responding based on a hunch or guess or 'felt' sense of a feeling or feelings.

Now we will look in detail at them all.

Zero empathy

In a coaching situation, while caring for your client, you may be inadvertently offering zero empathy by judging your client, offering them advice, and questioning them. Judgement, advice and questioning are not empathy, though they do have their place. On the other hand, you may find yourself losing interest in your client due to boredom, fatigue with a repeated story or simple dislike of their values.

Zero empathy may also be silent. As a coach you may recognize in your client a feeling which is recognized by yourself and you might even imagine you are being empathic. If you do not respond to your client, you have not offered empathy even when your face and body are mirroring your client. Mirroring is known to establish connection and build relationship, so it is useful in coaching but it is not a complete expression of empathy.

You may be offering zero empathy if you are distracted as the manager, texting on his phone in Figure 1.1 while his employee is weeping.

Figure 1.1   Zero empathy

Partial empathy

Partial empathy is a form of empathy which attends to only part of your client's emotional world. For example, your client may be expressing, in words, their frustration with a new ordering system and their intention to apply for promotion, while their voice is sounding wobbly. Your partial empathic response recognizes their feeling of frustration and the reason for it, saying: 'This new system seems confusing but it is time to move on' (Figure 1.2). This fulfils the three components of empathy mentioned earlier, i.e. a feeling (confusing), a reason for it, and telling the person about it. However, it is partial because it does not include the emotion revealed in your client's 'wobbly' voice, which suggests anxiety and lack of confidence. This second feeling is the one which may inhibit your client from significant action rather than their confusion. So partial empathy is good enough but not enough for major change.

Figure 1.2 Partial empathy

Primary empathy

Primary empathy is a response which includes recognition of all the feelings expressed by your client, the reasons for these feelings, and a response which identifies them accurately. For primary empathy as a coach, you will respond only to feelings which have been expressed either in words or non-verbally by your client. For example, a response to the client above could be: 'You are finding the new system confusing and you are thinking of going for promotion but you don't sound confident about it' (Figure 1.3).

Figure 1.3   Primary empathy

The test for primary empathy is evidence, either verbal or non-verbal of the feeling or feelings the coach has identified.

Advanced empathy

Advanced empathy is a response for which there may not be sufficient evidence. Here as coach, you are making a hunch about a possible feeling in your client and you could be mistaken. This is sometimes described as a 'felt sense'. An advanced empathic response to the client above, based on previous conversations, might be: 'This new system seems confusing, you're concerned about your career and you might go for promotion. I know you're upset about X being promoted when you have been working such long hours – you must have felt betrayed when X went for the same job and got it. No wonder you don't feel all that confident now about applying' (Figure 1.4).

Figure 1.4 Advanced empathy

Because advanced empathy is based on unexpressed feelings, the client may respond with 'Actually that's not it, it's more…' and their real feelings will emerge. Alternatively they will agree: 'Thank you, that's exactly how it is' and the coaching begins.

In summary, primary empathy responds to feelings and experience which have been expressed explicitly, while advanced empathy endeavours to 'read between the lines' or responds to feelings which may have been expressed obliquely. In the typical organization the work culture tends to devalue feeling and emotion and clients may not express their feelings clearly. Advanced empathy skills may be called for where your client is suppressing or denying what they are really feeling. This is particularly important when you are dealing with conflict, or when it is necessary to challenge or confront your client.

You may have noticed that the missing feelings in Figures 1.1, 1.2 and 1.3 are often seen as negative, i.e. distress, anxiety and lack of confidence. The popular approach to happiness and success known as positive psychology recommends focusing primarily or even solely, on what goes well, i.e. positive feelings. However, Tali Sharot, in *The Optimism Bias* (2012), suggests that ignoring the negatives in life can lead to insecurity, uncertainty and unhappiness. More about this can be found in Oliver Burkeman's book, *The Antidote: Happiness for People Who Can't Stand Positive Thinking* (2012). Burkeman argues that the global industry of positive thinking with its constant efforts to eliminate the negative, itself leads to insecurity and uncertainty. He suggests that the positive thinking practitioners trying to make everything right leads to the reverse, as seeking happiness ironically reduces your chances of achieving it. An approach which includes both positive and negative feelings is more realistic and less likely to lead to failure and depression.

Modes of empathy

Clients will express emotions which they have felt in the past, or they are feeling in the present or indeed, what they are likely to feel in the future. So empathy may be offered in three modes:

Past   Present   Future

Let's take a look at how these modes work in a coaching situation.

An ability to work in all three modes enables a coach to identify and respond to the emotional element in any future actions as well as present and past feelings. For example, your client may be preparing for an important presentation to the board. They have feelings of fear (in the present) based on unhappy experiences with presentations (in the past, and the potential feelings when actually presenting (in the future) are likely to be nervousness and fear.

A case study will show this scenario in action.

Martina, an executive coach

Martina has been commissioned to work with Brian, the operations director in a global retail organization. Martina has already established a good relationship with Brian and they have agreed his objectives, one of which is to deal with his terror of presentations. Martina begins by saying: 'Tell me about your presentation.' Her empathy recognizes the unhappy feelings in the past. She says: 'Your last presentation didn't go well and you felt awful.' Her questioning will explore what happened to Brian on that occasion and other similar events.

Thereafter, Martina recognizes her client's current feelings of fear about his presentation, saying: 'You're feeling afraid of it happening again.' This is followed by a discussion about the event.

Finally, Martina will attend to her client's potential feelings of nervousness at the presentation itself, saying: 'It sounds like you may feel apprehensive before it.' Martina works with Brian to expand his range of feelings around presentations. These are likely to include excitement, confidence and hope. They also agree on a plan for a practice run.

Empathy in all three modes can support further techniques like rehearsal and visioning.

Why is empathy necessary?

For empathy to be effective, it must be received by your client to be any use for learning and change. Why should this be? The use of empathy uncovers the hidden elements in people which limit their ability to learn and change. What are these elements? Young children are enthusiastic learners and are ready to learn everything without limits. So what happens? Young children encounter first their parents or carers, then family, school, teachers, friends, etc. Figure 1.5 shows how experience affects life.

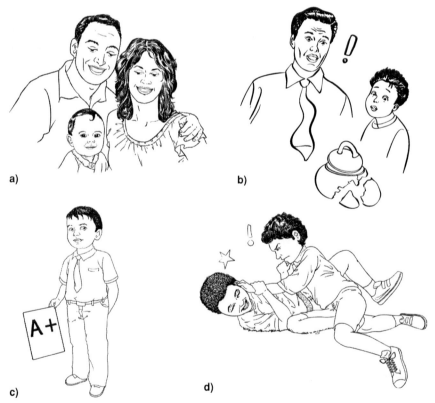

Figure 1.5   a) New arrival!, b) Oh dear!, c) Well done!, d) Grrr!!

The Top Secret File and the locked trunk

Every encounter affects us emotionally, negatively or positively. When feelings are discouraged or forbidden, we hide them so that we will continue to be loved. Hence, as adults, we carry a Top Secret File containing our hidden feelings. These are feelings which, as children, we learnt to hide as they led to disapproval. These feelings may include:

- *Anger* – some families cannot tolerate conflict and any expression of anger by a boy or girl is discouraged or punished. Girls particularly may learn to hide their expression of anger as they are encouraged to be 'nice'.
- *Hurt and sadness* – many children are encouraged to hide their tears, especially if they are boys and they are told to learn to have a stiff upper lip.
- *Fear of failure* – this may be actively discouraged in high-achieving families.
- *Love of physical fun and exercise and mischief.*

We also drag behind us a locked trunk containing feelings which are so unacceptable that they are actually forgotten. These may include fear, jealousy, resentment, hate, shame, and deep sadness. To become aware of these forgotten feelings is too awful to contemplate except within the safety of therapy. Coaching is able to address what is in the Top Secret File but is not suitable to deal with what is in the locked trunk (Figure 1.6).

Figure 1.6   The Top Secret File and the locked trunk

There is nothing to be ashamed of here, it is the human condition, everybody has a Top Secret File and a locked trunk that they are unwilling to share with others. But how does it affect the ability to change? Let's meet Jason and see how his Top Secret File and his locked trunk have affected him.

Jason

Jason was an only child, and had a rather strict upbringing. His father died when he was just a boy and his mother was protective and insisted that Jason should be careful about outdoor activities like sports and playing in the street. Jason has tended to be quiet and bookish rather than active and sociable. As a child he received messages about being too boisterous and he learnt to hide his desire for games.

Jason, the adult, trained as a chartered accountant and is now a success-ful senior partner in a global consultancy. He tends to be rather serious in his work and finds the informality of his young team somewhat disturbing. They mistake his reserve for disapproval and tease him unmercifully.

Jason attends a management development programme for senior part-ners where he meets an executive coach, Rebecca. As part of the pro-gramme he receives one-to-one sessions with Rebecca. Through Rebecca's use of empathy they quickly form a relationship of trust and Jason talks about his management style.

He tells Rebecca how much he disapproves of his team horsing around at work. Rebecca says: 'You don't like to see these youngsters playing around and you feel uncomfortable.'

Jason says: 'I have never liked that sort of behaviour – I was brought up to keep myself to myself.'

Rebecca says: 'That must have been lonely,' and Jason says, rather sadly, 'Yes, it was – I never had fun, you know.'

The coaching continues with questions and a discussion about what fun is appropriate in the workplace. Jason's fear of having noisy fun is in his Top Secret File and is kept there because he learnt that this was how to be Jason the good boy. What he learns in coaching is that the fear of having noisy fun is not serving Jason the adult. It is easy to imagine this is a simple thing for him to do but the fear is powerful and Jason will need courage to overcome his fear and risk joining in with some of his team's activities. The Top Secret File serves to protect and defend Jason so that he can present himself in a way he has learnt over time is socially acceptable. However, the hidden feelings can be found when empathy is offered to him in a safe relationship.

What if your client is denying their deep feelings? These are likely to be in their locked trunk and they may be addressed in therapy if your client wishes. We discuss the boundary between coaching and therapy in Chapter 8.

How does empathy lead to change?

Working with your client effectively, the objective of your interaction will be some form of change for the client. That change will be a result of the client recognizing that their future stance towards a situation is going to be different from how it is now. That difference from 'now' will be a result of some form of learning on the part of your client. This is where empathy can support the change.

3-D learning: the three domains of learning

When adults learn, develop and change, they do so by a combination of what we call 3-D learning, using the three domains of learning. These three domains are knowing, doing and feeling. Naturally a skilled person uses all three in concert rather than separately as explained below.

Knowledge has been linked traditionally to thinking and thinking-based learning is shown in Figure 1.7 a).

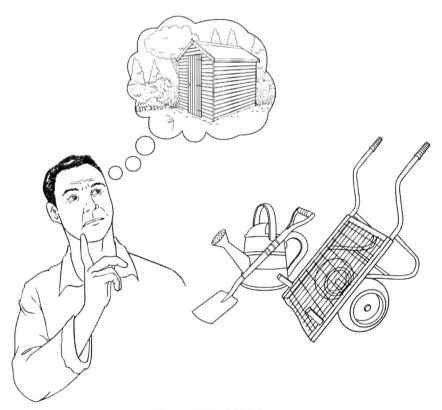

Figure 1.7   a) Thinking

People use thinking-based learning in order to get more *knowledge* – this will be familiar to you from school or college at these levels:

- beginning with facts (like times tables or an idea for a shed);
- an ability to understand a process (like equations or what is needed to build a shed);
- an ability to combine what you know (like applying this to costs) and later to evaluate results.

Feeling-based learning is largely absent from traditional theories of learning and has only recently appeared in management development with the advent of EQ. Feeling-based learning is shown in Figure 1.7 b) where the task seems daunting.

Figure 1.7 b) Feeling

Feeling-based learning is recognition and maybe alteration in *how you feel* about events, yourself and other people, and this may come about by meeting an inspiring teacher or manager, with sometimes dramatic results.

- The feeling domain begins with receiving (when you become aware of your own or other's feelings).
- It then develops into an ability to respond to them (empathy), to value feelings, organize them and use them for learning.

Doing-based learning begins with creating a scale plan of the shed, shown in Figure 1.7 c).

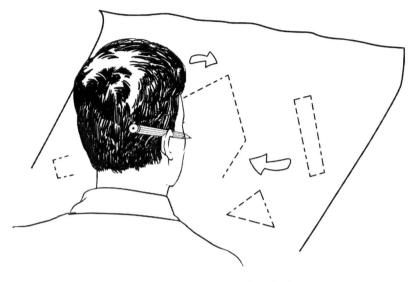

Figure 1.7 c) Doing (planning)

Doing-based learning becomes action which achieves the desired goal as in Figure 1.7 d).

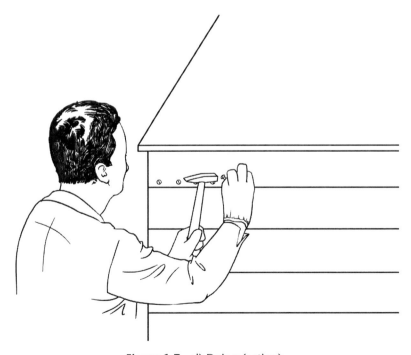

Figure 1.7 d) Doing (acting)

Doing-based learning is the very practical way of being able to *do things* by either copying an expert or following instructions, as in how to build a shed, for example:

- The action domain begins with seeing an objective (like the shed).
- Then, taking a position (with an initial plan).
- Developing this into an ability to respond (change materials or dimensions) and adapt to them.

There is additional feeling-based learning of satisfaction when the task is completed as in Figure 1.7 e).

Figure 1.7 e) Feeling

In addition, there may be a return to thinking-based learning when the shed is put to use. These three ways of learning: thinking, doing and feeling are all important, but coaching with empathy will focus particularly on feeling-based learning. Some business coaching has tended to focus on the knowing and doing domains, often to the neglect of the emotional domain. Why is knowing not enough?

Surely once your client understands what to do, all they have to do is get on with it? Learning is not a simple process and neither is change. Your client understands what is to be done, but finds it hard to do so. For instance your client may know all the details of a new ordering system and be able to describe it perfectly. This learning is knowing-based. However, he may feel resistant to using it, preferring the old method. If and when he feels differently, this is learning that is feeling-based. Once he adopts the new system and changes his behaviour to do so, his learning is action-based. All three are necessary, but the importance of the feeling-based learning is obvious as there is no change without it.

Human nature tends to resist change and those who work with people or organizations confirm that change is difficult, however much it is known to be a good thing. Learning which is knowing-based is needed, but thinking is not enough to make many of us change in ways that will meet the challenges of the modern world. Coaching with empathy uncovers the hidden emotions which are influencing our reaction to change. What evidence is there that empathy can achieve such a dramatic outcome?

Sixty years of research have consistently demonstrated that empathy is the most powerful determinant of client progress. Most of the evidence for empathy is found in reports of therapeutic work and outcomes. These include the following results:

- Clients learn to trust their own experience.
- Clients become less defensive, less risk-averse, less driven by 'oughts' and others' expectations.

As well as:

- Clients are able to be more honest with their colleagues, family and friends.

Our own practice-based evidence supports these statements and is the reason for this book.

Difficulties with empathy

If empathy is so effective, why isn't there more of it about and why isn't everyone doing it? There is a mixture of answers to this:

- Thoughts and feelings are mixed up for many people – they find it difficult to separate the two.
- The English language predisposes its speakers to judgement.
- Lack of emotional language – see Chapter 4.
- Multi-relationships: Organizations are complex and relationships within it are complex also. For every individual there is their intra-personal relationship; their interpersonal relationships with countless others; and their relationship with the organization.
- People resist demands but respond well to requests and declared needs from individuals or the organization.
- The assumption (or reality) that the organizational needs will conflict with individual needs.
- Emotions are perceived as a sign of weakness – hence embarrassment.
- Lack of self-empathy which is linked to other-empathy and ultimately the empathic organization.
- Emotion is invisible in a culture which prioritizes thought and action.

What empathy is NOT

It is important to be clear in a coaching relationship that empathy is NOT:

- *Questioning*: the temptation to get more information is strong. As a coach you may believe that with just a few more details you will be able to solve your client's difficulty. You may also have a hidden statement or advice in your question.
- *Agreement*: this is the one most managers fear. To respond to a person's feelings is not to agree with the reasons for those feelings. Someone may feel angry with their manager's treatment – empathy does not condone angry behaviour.
- *Being nice*: you may hesitate to offer empathy for fear of appearing too nice when you need to be assertive.
- *Being weak or permissive*: when you want to be firm and assertive.
- *Interpretation*: for coaches with a psychology background, this is a real temptation. Client behaviour can be categorized into denial, displacement, neediness, etc. and you may be tempted to share your insights with your client.
- *Inaccuracy*: use your listening skills as you may not have heard your client properly.
- *Parroting*: over-use of the same language
- *Sympathy*: feeling sorry for your client.
- *Giving advice*.
- *Giving evaluation*: that's good or that's bad are both evaluations.
- *Giving an opinion*: what you think may be relevant but it's not empathy.
- *Making a judgement*: ditto.
- *Not challenging*: empathy can be challenging if the relationship is robust enough to carry it.
- *Criticizing*: what you think may be relevant – may not be of interest to your client.

Each of these responses has its place in coaching but none of them is empathic.

How can empathy benefit an organization?
The business case for coaching with empathy

Return on Investment (ROI) has been linked to how engaged employees are in a business, and research in the UK has identified the feeling domain as a key part of engagement. When employees are allowed to have 'the freedom to voice ideas to which managers listen', this is one of the main drivers of engagement (Robinson et al. 2004). In addition, the feeling domain is one of the three ingredients in positive engagement which is defined as: 'being positively present during the performance of work by willingly contributing intellectual effort, experiencing positive emotions and meaningful connections to others' (CIPD 2010b).

Empathy has a role to play here, as until negative emotions are voiced and accepted, the positive ones remain hidden or non-existent. Some coaches believe that ignoring negative emotions will make them go away. Unfortunately psychology does not support this expectation and people persist in trying to have their sometimes quite simple negative emotions like boredom or impatience accepted and understood. This does not mean that coaches must agree with their client about the reasons for their feelings. For example, you can accept and understand your client's impatience for promotion without agreeing that they have been unfairly held back or that they are just not up to it.

Evidence suggests that engaged employees have an enormous impact on the organization's performance. Flatter and less hierarchal organizations are increasingly aware that telling people what to do is not effective for engaging them with the organization's aims. However, this engagement cannot be forced – it is not something which appears in an employment contract. Coaching can generate engagement by using empathy.

Engagement requires the three kinds of learning mentioned earlier: knowing-based learning, feeling-based learning and action-based learning. When coaching includes empathy, staff engagement is more likely to follow and for developmental coaching empathy is essential. The introduction of EQ is an example of knowing-based learning which is ineffective. Many CEOs and directors can tell you all about EQ when there may be little evidence of empathy in their organizations. Their learning is knowing-based not feeling-based so there is less likely to be a change in behaviour.

Empathy works to help the organization to include feeling-based learning as well as action and knowledge, by revealing, first, the taken-for-granteds or tfgs in a system, and, second, by revealing the power horizon.

Swimming in the tfgs

Tfgs are those conditions and assumptions that are unstated yet have an influence over how the organization operates. The taken-for-granteds (tfgs) in any organization are invisible to employees who are like fish in water who don't know they are in water. For instance, assumptions exist about age, gender, etc. such as 'old people don't have sex' and 'men are brutes' or 'women are emotional'. An example of an invisible tfg is the assumption that the coach must be an expert in a particular field in order to be able to coach others.

Adam

Adam, supervisor of a team of part-time sales assistants assumes that his sales assistants are not interested in self-development so he doesn't include them in the training schedule. Adam carries an invisible tfg, where the assumption is that employees at certain grades are not interested in self-development or promotion.

When clients can discuss honestly what they know or don't know, what they have done or will do, and how they feel about it, they are likely to be able to challenge the tfgs, and find their personal power. Sometimes parts of the tfgs are out of sight for clients as they are beyond the power horizon.

The power horizon

David Smail, an English psychologist, argues in *The Nature of Unhappiness* (2001) that power in society is partly responsible for personal distress. He describes the power horizon as those forces which control our lives that are 'completely out of sight' but which we 'can do nothing about'. This is indeed true. However, there are also those forces which are nearer to us but appear equally out of sight, kept in position by tfgs.

> Some of Adam's team may assume they are not suitable for promotion or development as they are never offered training. This mirrors Adam's assumption that because they are young women, they are likely to leave to look after their family and the training would not benefit the company. They, in their turn, then tend to view themselves as limited in their abilities without seeing the power horizon in position here, which is actually a reduced training budget which staff know nothing about as well as Adam's stance towards his married women staff which he has learnt to keep to himself.

Within the power horizon the real power is kept invisible particularly to those who are powerless. For example, it is not unusual to hear managers state that their employees are not interested in promotion and development, often due to budget concerns. The employees tends to view themselves as described above.

As a coach you can enable a client to become aware of tfgs in their nearby power horizon through empathy. Once a tfg is recognized, the employee can have a view about how to respond to it.

Can an organization be empathic?

Dev Patnaik, an American strategy consultant, in his book, *Wired to Care* (2009), shows that the empathic organization connects with its customers far more effectively than others. When employees experience a personal *human* connection to their business task, they engage and do their best. Patnaik and his partners have published numerous instances of empathy in the organization that has led to better products, more employee engagement, better customer feedback and increased revenues. He describes a major flaw in contemporary business practice as a lack of empathy inside large corporations. Patnaik argues that corporate personnel believe they understand their business on the basis of quantitative data and ignore the feeling element in their customer relationships. Business has been diagnosed as being stuck in two dimensions: thinking and doing with employees, managers and leaders 'choking on thought'. The recent global economic crisis must give us pause to consider how appropriate our systems are for safety, security and the well-being of people and the planet.

Patnaik claims that the real opportunity for companies doing business in the twenty-first century is to create a widely held sense of empathy for customers. Such institutions, he claims, see new opportunities more quickly than competitors, adapt to change more easily, and create workplaces that offer employees a greater sense of mission in their jobs.

In her (2011) book, *The Empathy Factor*, organizational consultant Marie Miyashiro also argues the value of bringing empathy to the workplace, and describes it as competitive advantage. She suggests that connections in corporate life do not meet the needs of those who work there and this affects productivity, services and profits alike. Empathy in the workplace results in lower costs, improved productivity, less accidents and absenteeism, and increased revenue, profit and stock market value (Miyashiro 2011: 29).

There is proof that empathy works like this from Gallup data and leadership research. Gallup polls consistently identify the desired qualities of leaders as trust, compassion, honesty, integrity and respect. For organizations, empathy works in teams and individuals. Teams with leaders who generate respect are more successful than those which don't. Gallup data identify leaders who demonstrate honesty and sensitivity as most effective especially when they combine these qualities with the ability to ensure that the job gets done and problems are solved (Gallup 2008).

Summary

In this chapter we explain what empathy is, in four levels and three modes, and what it is not. We have shown how empathy helps learning and change, by including feelings as well as thinking and doing. Empathy stimulates change and reduces a client's immunity to change, through accessing their Top Secret File. Finally we have reported some of the benefits to organizations which include empathy in their interactions.

2   Empathy in situational coaching

In this chapter we describe four different coaching situations: performance, engagement, development and systemic. The situations are different because they have different purposes, the desired changes are different, so the coaching approach is different in each one. Empathy is effective in each situation if you use it at the correct level and mode. In this chapter we describe how to use empathy in each of the four situations shown in Figure 2.1.

Figure 2.1   Situational coaching

For many people, coaching is simply coaching and the situation is not relevant. Surely all coaching is the same? The nature of your coaching will depend on the situation in which the coaching is taking place. The situation defines the coaching. To identify what type of coaching is required in each situation, you may find it helpful to ask yourself some questions about it:

- Whose objectives is the coaching for? Is it the organization or the individual? Or is it both?
- What is the hoped-for change? Is it improvement or a big change – a transformation?
- Which coaching approach is to be used? Will you give advice or avoid telling your client what to do?

These situational questions will dictate the type of coaching on offer and the range of objectives and change are shown in Figure 2.2.

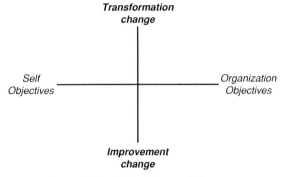

Figure 2.2   Objectives and change

Figure 2.2 shows two dimensions: the coaching objectives and the kind of change the coaching is for.

- *From left to right:* This is the objectives dimension, from self objectives to organization objectives.
- *From top to bottom:* This is the change dimension from complete transformation to improvement. Coaching which is for improving performance is nearer to organization objectives and further away from transformation. Coaching for engagement begins to include the self objectives but is still for improvement. Coaching for personal or professional development is near to self objectives and also transformation change. Systemic change is near to organization objectives and also transformation change.

The four different situations are shown again in Figure 2.3.

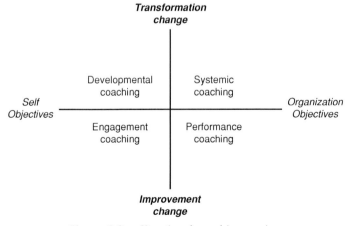

Figure 2.3   Situational coaching again

You can recognize your coaching situation by what change is desired and by whom. When you have identified the situation in which you are coaching, then you can decide on the best approach and how to use empathy. We explain situational coaching through coaching in one multinational retail organization, N&T. The organization chart is shown in Figure 2.4.

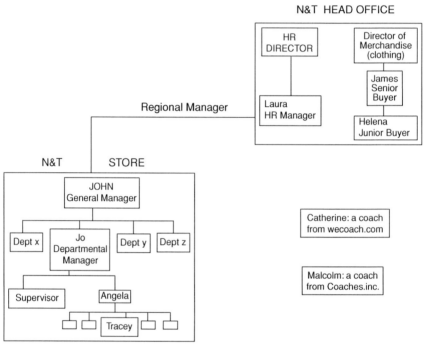

Figure 2.4   Extract from N&T organization chart

The sponsors of the coaching, the coaches, the clients and employees are as follows:

- Jo: departmental manager
- James: senior buyer at head office
- Helena: junior buyer at head office and member of James' team
- John: Jo's store manager
- Laura: HR manager at head office
- Angela: supervisor and Jo's direct report
- Tracey: one of Angela's sales team
- Catherine: James' coach
- Malcolm: John's coach

Each of these four situations – performance coaching, engagement coaching, developmental coaching and systemic coaching – calls for different approaches to coaching as the objectives and change are different in each. Different situations need different coaching.

Types of coaching

Performance coaching

The coaching objective is improved performance from staff. The objective is owned by the organization and the coaching method may include giving advice. Managers use coaching to improve business performance. A line manager may be trained to coach their staff or a team leader may be trained to coach their team. In this situation the coaching is aiming at improved performance by employees for the benefit of the business.

> #### Jo
>
> Jo joined N&T, a multinational retail company, as a management trainee straight from university. N&T is one of the UK's leading retailers with annual operating profits of over £500,000,000, and 20,000,000 customers a year. Jo has a degree in Retail Management which included interpersonal skills training so she sailed through the selection centre. She has done the usual placements around the business and has just received her first position as a departmental manager in a city centre store. She will manage ten sales staff and two supervisors in the lingerie department. Jo reports to the general manager, John. The sales targets for Jo's department are already set down and she will achieve them through performance management of her staff.

Engagement coaching

The coaching objective is again improved performance with something more. Engagement means that the staff are committed to the mission of the organization and their part in achieving it. So engagement coaching aims to persuade employees to adopt the objectives of the organization, or align their own objectives with those of the organization. Line managers are most likely to deliver engagement coaching but a coach may be brought in from outside to work with a manager or team to increase staff engagement with company aims.

> #### James
>
> James holds a senior buyer position in N&T and reports to the director of merchandise (clothing) at head office. He comes with experience of his family's business in the East End of London and is highly regarded by the board. James heads up a team of young junior buyers, most of whom are fashion or design graduates. They are wildly enthusiastic but have little experience of business and James finds that they can often get so carried away by a new and exciting

line of clothing that they forget to keep procurement within budget. The objectives for James' section include a strong price architecture, efficiency across the supply chain and better sourcing and economies of scale to retain budget discipline. James wants to get his team engaged in the needs of the business.

Developmental coaching

The coaching objective belongs to the individual being coached. They seek transformational change for themselves through internal or external coaching and their objectives may or may not be aligned with the organization's objectives. In an organization, executive coaching may be used to support a promising employee or senior staff to reach their full potential for the benefit of the business.

John

John is the general manager of one of N&T's flagship stores, and responsible for 80 staff and a turnover of over £1,000,000 per week. He is capable and competent in financial matters, but tends to micromanage his departmental heads. His regional manager works with John to identify what will make him even more effective in his work. Together they identify John's rather directive style and his reluctance to delegate. They agree to commission an external executive coach for John.

Systemic coaching

The fourth corner is the organizational context where a coaching culture can support systemic change and potential transformation. The organization aims to transform itself through developmental coaching by internal or external coaches.

Laura

Laura is the HR manager at N&T head office. She reports to the HR director and is given a fairly free hand for the learning and development function. The company has resolved to create a coaching culture in the organization and she is aware that the steps to achieve this include:

- coaches for executive directors and senior managers;
- coach training for general and departmental managers;
- coaching appears as an item in appraisals;
- coaching as a management skill in all management development;
- all HR staff are to be trained in coaching;
- a coaching approach is used with suppliers.

Laura is an important change agent in the company. Her director has given her a target: a complete culture change throughout the business.

Coaching those at the top of an organization is recommended by some as the best way to create a coaching culture. However, evidence for improved organizational performance actually identifies the engagement of staff as a key factor. Enhanced engagement of staff has been statistically linked to improved financial performance of the organization. A coaching culture in an organization where there is coaching at all levels is thought to support transformation although evidence for this is tentative. Transformation here means a preferred organizational change as declared in organizational aims or expressed by the individual client.

Asking the question about coaching objectives will clarify what kind of coaching is needed. Some managers may assume that all coaching of staff is performance coaching. Executive coaches may assume that all coaching is developmental. Where the coaching aims for more engagement from staff, development may occur through the coaching itself. Systemic change needs a coaching culture to support it and robust measures to evaluate it.

Coaching in the different situations

We now consider coaching in each of the four different situations by examining objectives, desired change and the different empathy needed for each.

Performance coaching

The purpose of performance management is clear – it addresses the goals of the organization, whether these coincide with those of employees or not. Performance management aims to help people to understand how their work contributes to the goals of the organization. Performance coaching should ensure that the right skills and effort are focused on the things that really matter to the organization. Performance coaching aims to make an impact on the organization's achievements.

Performance objectives

The organization needs to manage the performance of its employees through effective line management. As the organization dictates the objectives of the coaching, employees do not choose objectives for themselves. Performance coaching occurs when the manager is seeking to improve the performance of their staff to achieve the organization's objectives.

Jo

Jo runs the lingerie department in a busy store with ten sales staff. She is new to the area, having transferred from another store after her promotion. She has been presented with tough sales targets without much consultation. The bad weather has led to a decrease in customer footfall and she has missed her weekly target twice. The targets cannot be changed and Jo decides to try coaching her staff in the way she has been trained by the external executive coaching company.

Performance change

Performance coaching aims for staff to adjust their behaviour to deliver the required objectives of the organization.

> Performance coaching is part of Jo's role as departmental manager. As manager, Jo's brief is improved performance by her staff, in line with the sales targets of the organization. As a line manager Jo must meet company objectives, indeed her own position depends on it. Her staff have no choice as their job depends on it. Quite sensibly they accept the company objectives to keep their job and their income.

Jo is looking for improvement in staff performance without changing what she wants them to do. She wants the staff to improve their weekly sales. Improved performance by her staff is the change he is looking for. How will Jo coach her staff?

Performance coaching approach (Jo and Angela)

For performance coaching, traditionally, managers would tell their staff what to do. This is increasingly unacceptable in today's work environments. However, performance coaching focuses on efficiency and objective targets or standards, very much needed in day-to-day work. The approach aims at improved performance, how to do the job better, in line with organizational goals.

> When Jo received coach training, she was encouraged to avoid telling her staff what to do and instead to question them about their performance. Open questions were recommended. So as sales were below target, Jo started by asking one of her team, slightly testily, 'How are you going to achieve your weekly sales target?' and was surprised by a blank response.

When Jo discussed this at her next session with her executive coach, the discussion focused on empathy and how she might use it with her staff. Next day she tried again with another member of staff, Angela, beginning with an invitation.

> Jo wanted the report of sales performance to come from Angela so she asked: 'How did we do on sales last week, Angela?' Her reply was: 'It's a shame it hasn't been achieved this week and the company needs to revise it plans.' Angela expressed two feelings, disappointment (in her words) and impatience with the company (in her voice). As a busy manager, Jo has little time for extended conversations which include all the feelings of her staff. Her focus is improved performance and she has already used her assertive skills

to make this clear. Now Jo, drawing on her training, offered partial empathy, i.e. she responded only to feelings which were relevant to the task in hand. She said: 'You seem disappointed', leaving Angela's impatience with the company aside, as this is not appropriate for performance coaching. Angela's reaction to Jo's partial empathy was: 'Yes, the weather didn't help...we tried to encourage people to buy for Valentine's Day.' Jo followed up with 'What do you think might help?' and the coaching conversation identified a plan for Angela to focus on one particular line as the weather improved.

Choosing to respond to one feeling and leave the other alone is an example of partial empathy explained earlier. It is important to be clear about this when you are coaching at work, as for either engagement or development, you will coach using empathy in a different way.

Questions in performance coaching

As a performance coach, you will need to question the employee concerned to check that they understand the significance of sales targets to meet performance objectives. However, employees may harbour negative reactions to the performance targets presented to them, for reasons which may include boredom, frustration and stress as well as a potential clash of values where the employee is not happy with the purposes of their organization.

Tracey

Tracey is an intelligent teenager who is one of Angela's sales team in the lingerie department. She didn't quite make her grades to study sociology at university and decided to work in retail. Her romance with a school friend led to an early marriage and children so she works part-time to fit in with her young family. Tracey finds that the work on the sales floor can be boring and when her children are unwell, she feels anxious and distracted. She has little interest in the departmental sales targets as her weekly wage remains the same whatever the business does. She is also rather shocked to find tiny bikinis for little girls being sold in the swimwear department. She has values which include disapproval of dressing children in provocative clothing.

As her team leader in this situation, Angela focuses only on the feelings which affect Tracey's performance. When Angela asks Tracey about last week's sales, Tracey says: 'I have a four-year-old at home with a temperature, and anyway what difference will it make to me?' Using partial empathy, Angela responds: 'You feel distracted because your little girl is unwell today, you must be anxious about her.' When Tracey agrees, Angela may be able to consider altering Tracey's hours as a temporary measure. She leaves the feelings about wages and the values of the company alone.

If Angela is tempted to engage in higher levels of empathy when doing performance coaching, she may find herself straying into a different coaching context. Hence the key skills in performance coaching are questioning and partial empathy.

Engagement coaching

Employees are engaged when they are committed to the organization and its values. Engagement can be seen as a willingness to help out colleagues. The important thing is that engagement cannot be required as part of the employment contract as it comes voluntarily from the employee. Engaged employees are willing employees with positive emotions about their work and good connections with their colleagues. Research shows that engaged employees are more productive and this affects organizational performance (Gallup 2010). Line managers are most likely to deliver engagement coaching, although increasingly external practitioners are involved in engagement work.

Engagement coaching objectives

Engagement coaching occurs where a senior manager or leader is seeking more commitment from employees. The coaching aims to persuade employees to either adopt the objectives of the organization, or align their own objectives with the organization's mission. As engagement is not part of an employment contract, engagement coaches are likely to use coaching techniques like active listening and empathy as well as questioning and feedback, rather than giving advice or telling staff what to do.

James

James is the senior buyer at head office in the same company as Jo. He was appointed for his knowledge and experience in the clothing sector, having run his own business for years. He is responsible for a team of talented junior buyers who respect his experience but think he's a bit old-fashioned. He continues to wear a suit when his young staff are in tee shirts. He needs them to be engaged with their work to be successful in procurement within budget, to meet the objectives of the company. There have been a number of disagreements about the Spring collection and James has been sent on a coaching course. When he coaches his team, he is seeking to persuade them to engage as much as possible with company aims and, if possible, align them with their own. The company aims to offer a line in lingerie which will result in increased year-on-year sales. As the coaching objectives are owned by the organization in the person of James, the members of his team are not the true owners of the coaching objectives.

Engagement change

Organizations aim to stimulate commitment in their staff by persuading them to align some of the organization's objectives with their own so that they work hard without being told. In the factsheet provided by the CIPD in 2010, engagement is described as:

> Commitment to the organization and its values and a willingness to help out colleagues (organizational citizenship). It goes beyond job satisfaction and is not simply motivation. Engagement is not something the employee has to offer. It cannot be required as part of the employment contract.
>
> (CIPD 2010a: 1)

This recognizes that employees have choices and can decide what level of engagement to offer the employer. However, there is also evidence from research undertaken by Kingston Business School that engaged employees deliver improved business performance. In addition, the research quotes that engagement has an emotional element, as the results suggest that engaged employees are 'positively present during the performance of work by willingly contributing intellectual effort, experiencing positive emotions and meaningful connections to others' (CIPD 2010b: 5).

> In his role as senior buyer at head office, James tries to use coaching to persuade his staff to adopt the company's aim which is to refresh the company's lingerie offer as their own without blowing the budget. One of his team, Helena, has a tendency to over-purchase new and fashionable lines. The change James wants here is that Helena is committed to refreshing the lingerie range in line with company policy and within budget. Helena has a degree in fashion and, new to the job, is very enthusiastic about new ideas for lingerie, not always keeping her eye on the budget.

Engagement coaching has some factors in common with performance in that the desired change is improvement for the employee without personal development. To achieve this James needs to offer coaching which should be limited to primary empathy. Primary empathy is used in this situation because the company objectives may not be accepted by his staff and the alternative method of persuasion is applied.

This type of approach is used mostly by line managers in organizations. This is not quite as devious as it sounds. Many employees are able to assess what they are being asked to do, compare this with their own needs and desires, and become engaged with organizational aims. A coaching approach which includes primary empathy acknowledges the employee's own feelings, hopes and fears, as well as those of the organization. A line manager with the ability to coach in this way can deliver employee engagement.

Engagement coaching approach (James and Helena)

The Kingston Business School research also established that the way managers behave contributes significantly towards engagement. Managers' behaviour is identified in a recent NICE report as contributing to employee well-being at work (NICE 2009). Engagement coaching should include primary empathy before questioning, as intrusive questioning before empathy tends to 'switch off' an employee.

How does James coach to persuade Helena?

> James has been encouraged to use questioning rather than telling his staff what to do. When Helena comes to tell him about her latest line order, she says: 'James, I have managed to source those really stunning sets from Thailand – the ones you saw at the design stage.' She adds that the purchase has unfortunately take the section over budget.
>
> James begins his coaching with an open question. 'How can you ensure that your purchasing remains within budget?' and Helena responds: 'Look, do you want my ideas or not?'

James' question addresses the thinking element in change but not the emotional factors which influence it so powerfully.

> However, if, before his question, James offers empathy at primary level by saying: 'You were really excited about this new line and then you realized that you had gone over budget. Oh dear, that's disappointing for you. We are lucky to have your ideas, Helena, and we need to look at how we can keep within budget and still use them.' Then, Helena visibly relaxes, feels understood and is more ready to work with the problem. His questions will follow and a discussion and agreement about what to do.
>
> James has recognized Helena's feelings and experience while at the same time maintaining a focus on the organization's objectives.

Questions in engagement coaching

Questioning and empathy are the two skills which tend to be used for engagement but often in the wrong order. Empathy followed by questioning is a better method for building an engagement relationship with an employee or client. Some coach training encourages coaches to offer empathy to help persuade but don't often give any help on how to do this. As an engagement coach you want to offer primary empathy in response to your client's feelings. If you are unable to identify a feeling, beware the temptation to pose the 'How does that make you feel?' question (HDTMYF?), or worse, the 'how do you feel?' question (HFYF?).

The HDTMYF? or HDYF? question is a development one and assumes that you have the requisite empathic skill to respond to the answer. This means that you must be able to respond to feelings of desperation, depression, rage and grief, or even suicidal urges. You may find that your client presents feelings about a subject where as a coach you do not feel competent to deal with them.

> When James is unable to identify Helena's feelings, he resorts to HDYF? and is horrified when she bursts into tears. She manages to tell him that she finds criticism very difficult at the moment as she is recovering from a termination and hasn't told her parents. James has blundered into a coaching context for which he has not been trained and refers her to HR.

Many people working in business have learned to be unaware of their feelings, and if they are, they are not encouraged to express them. The two questions HDTMYF? and HDYF? may meet with outright denial or a disclosure for which you do not feel competent. We discuss how to deal with both in Chapter 8.

Empathy should precede open questioning to promote engagement and empathy should be primary rather than advanced. Primary empathy is appropriate for engagement as the employee has no choice about their objectives. Pursuing their deeper feelings is a pointless exercise and may even lead to distress. This means that the coaching stays focused on the issue and how change can happen, rather than exploring deeper feelings.

Performance coaching and engagement coaching support efficiency and improved performance for the organization. Both are important for day-to-day business. However, organizations may wish to develop particular individuals for the benefit of the business and external coaches are often invited to work with such individuals using development coaching.

Development coaching

Development coaching happens when an expert coach is commissioned to work with an individual to realize their potential. The coaching change in development work is likely to be transformational for the individual concerned. The coach may be internal or external and in either case should be confidential. This means that the coach will not give information about the coaching to the organization.

Coaching will only lead to transformational development if the desire for change comes from your client themselves. Your client's objectives may or may not be aligned with the organization's objectives. An example of this was the coaching programme introduced for Sterling Bank managers in order to enlarge their offer to include selling financial services to their customers. Traditional bank managers were unable to align their objectives with those of the organization as they saw their role as being supportive and professional servants, not salesmen. The coaching resulted in a flood of resignations from the bank as the managers focused on their own objectives, i.e. to leave the company. (More details about Sterling Bank are given in our book, *Facilitating Reflective Learning in Coaching, Mentoring and Supervision*, second edition, 2012.)

Development coaching assumes that your client defines their own goals. Research shows that when a client decides on their coaching goals, they are more likely to achieve them. The organization is more likely to use the term 'executive coaching' for this kind of coaching.

Development objectives

John

John is the general manager of a large retail store with a high weekly turn-over. He has come up through the company, having joined as an assistant straight from school. He has a traditional management style and tends to over-manage the senior team. With the long hours in retail, he is showing signs of stress. However, he is successful and the company want to encourage his development. His regional manager believes that John has yet to realize his full potential and offers him coaching sessions with an external executive coach. John's regional manager has some inklings about John's management style but chooses to use the coaching budget, and an external coach, Catherine, a coach from wecoach.com to support him. John will create his own objectives which may or may not coincide with the company's.

The coaching objectives are primarily John's and the company are happy to invest in his development without imposing objectives, but trust that John's development will ultimately benefit the company.

Development change

Developmental change is driven by the client concerned and includes personal and professional issues, such as interpersonal skills, the work–life balance, delegation, dealing with conflict, -isms like sexism and racism, careers, relationships and values.

As general manager of the store concerned, John decides to use the coaching for his professional and personal development. For example, he decides to work on his ability to delegate, his ability to confront his colleagues and his work–life balance. They are likely to benefit the company but are not imposed, so change is possible with potential transformation for the manager concerned.

The kind of change which transforms attitudes and beliefs as well as behaviour requires that the client owns their objectives, that they have the power to achieve them, and that they are connected to others through empathy. Hence the changes which occur in developmental coaching are both personal and professional. Empathy has a part to play in both professional and personal matters. As his coach, Catherine offers an important model for John by demonstrating empathy in her coaching approach.

Development coaching approach

For development coaching, you are likely to be using a non-directive approach, where you start from the client's experience not your own. Empathy features early in development coaching followed by questioning, feedback and challenge. The quality of the relationship between you and your client is known to predict change which transforms their attitude, belief and behaviour. Both primary and advanced empathy are married to your other coaching skills to take your client to a new view of their world and potential transformation.

> John meets his coach, Catherine, and their first session is devoted to building the relationship and discussing potential objectives. John begins by saying: 'I'm not sure what coaching is', and Catherine uses empathy to build the relationship by saying: 'You're feeling unsure about this' and John says: 'Yes, I am. Is it like counselling?'
>
> Catherine resists the temptation to give him a lecture about coaching and instead says: 'You seem rather rushed – tell me about your job.'
>
> He says: 'There is so much to do – sometimes I just don't know where to start.' Catherine says: 'You sound a bit pressured – tell me about it.' Eventually John admits to his difficulties with delegation and the stress he is experiencing. His first ideas focus on his problems with delegation, and these link to his issues around the work–life balance and stress.
>
> John describes how he manages his senior team. He describes his worry that his deputy will make a mistake and John will be blamed for it. He says with a worried look: 'What if Steve gets it wrong? I will carry the can for his mistake.'
>
> Catherine offers him primary empathy (based on John's facial expression and his words) saying: 'I guess you are afraid Steve will get it wrong and you will be held responsible.' John says: 'Yes, exactly, no wonder I'm careful.'
>
> Catherine then offers advanced empathy (based on what John has told her about himself) saying: 'John, you have high standards and you want your people to have them too. It must be difficult when they fall short of your standards.'
>
> When John moves towards what stops him changing his style, then Catherine, using advanced empathy, says: 'Perhaps you feel anxious when you leave your deputy in charge.' This is how empathy deals with John's emotional reaction (part of his Top Secret File) to the change he wants to make. He replies: 'Yes, I am anxious because Steve's failure is my failure and I can't have that.' Catherine then puts her first open question to John: 'What would happen if you failed?'
>
> Thereafter the session works with John's emotional reactions to potential failure, much of which was part of his upbringing and is getting in the way of him being able to delegate.

Doing development coaching or executive coaching

Development coaching may occur within the organization, with skilled in-house managers, inside the organization with external executive coaches, or outside the organization in a private arrangement. In doing development coaching you recognize and respect the real world of your client. This allows them to generate their own coaching purpose. As a development coach you respect your client's experience, and, by using advanced empathy you may enable them to move to potential transformation. Development coaching, more commonly called executive coaching, offers your client a chance to identify the tfgs in their environment, and challenge them. The process offers your client the potential for challenge and transformation, through a relationship which includes primary and advanced empathy. Development coaching, which includes advanced empathy has the potential to lead to change and transformation. Complications may arise if the organization is looking for engagement while the executive coach is aiming for developmental change. Part of contracting as an executive coach is helping a corporate client to understand what is and is not on offer.

Development coaching aims for a transformative change for an individual who generates their own objectives so the coaching is a voluntary choice by the client, not imposed on them by the organization. Clients are offered primary and advanced empathy and the relationship is the key to development and change. Clients are challenged and supported in whatever change they choose to make.

Expectations in coaching: keeping them realistic

The notion that coaching can meet all the needs of the client may lead to unrealistic expectations which may be shared by the coach, the client, the sponsor and the manager. The unrealistic expectation is that any kind of coaching can lead to personal or professional development as well as performance improvement and engagement. Therefore, being aware of the specific objectives of the coaching will lessen the chance of expectations becoming unrealistic.

When staff experience coaching as part of performance management, and their manager uses a different style for this, employees may imagine that the purpose is their personal development. The desired change is improved performance rather than developmental change. Managers should not be expected to apply development coaching in performance management situations. The change intended is improved performance measured by, say, increased sales not any kind of personal development. However, many managers (and their staff) may imagine that coaching will result in development change. The truth of this is shown in the comments below, from a senior manager, and trained coach, in a telecommunications company:

> The effectiveness of coaching in most large corporations is compromised by the organization's strong focus on achievement ... Managers are time-strapped. They therefore struggle to find the quality time needed to properly coach their staff, with the manager largely instructing the employee what to do as they can't afford the luxury of taking the time to help the employee to explore solutions for himself.
>
> In addition, due to the high pressure environment, there is little, if any, time to explore the employee's model of the world and take this into account

in their coaching sessions and discussions are largely 'matter of fact' and solution focused. The end result is that both the managers and their staff are left feeling disappointed and stressed.

(Brockbank and McGill 2012)

When coaching is used for performance management, managers and their staff should be informed about the objectives of the coaching. It is important for managers to be clear with their staff that coaching does not mean that their personal objectives will be considered. The coaching is provided to improve their performance in their job. Sometimes when engagement coaching occurs, employees may imagine that their development is the purpose.

Unrealistic expectations may be at work here so beware. The coaching sponsor, your client and the client organization may believe that performance or engagement coaching will lead to development and change. Although your client may align their own objective with those of the company, with engagement coaching, the coaching objective is still owned by the organization. Hence the change is likely to be limited to improvement. However, the coaching process itself may lead through engagement to development. When clients experience empathy, they are often motivated to further change and development.

As an external coach you need to be aware of the potential for unrealistic expectations. As a trained coach, you will be aware of the difference between your contractor, the HR manager, and the actual client. A three-way meeting is recommended before you proceed.

Laura

As HR manager, Laura has recruited an external coach, Malcolm, from coaches.inc to provide coaching in the retail organization mentioned above. She wants him to work with James, whose management style is rather traditional and paternal. This is not going down well with his young, talented and mainly female junior buyers. The company objectives include innovative design and budget discipline. To achieve the objectives of the organization, James is being asked to change his management style. At the meeting with HR and the coach, James is informed about the coaching objectives for him. He agrees to the coaching.

When James works with Malcolm, he experiences high quality coaching. Malcolm establishes a good relationship with James who has felt rather overlooked in the company; he listens to the reality of James who is struggling with the technology and the thinly disguised amusement of his team; and he offers James advanced empathy, saying: 'You must feel rather threatened by all these youngsters pushing their ideas at you.' James agrees and the coaching helps James to be more careful and resist saying, 'Calm down dear' to his female team members. For James, the change is transformational and has effects on his personal life and relationships with female members of his own family.

Systemic coaching

In this corner of our coaching matrix those leading the organization want it to transform itself. The route to effective transformation for an organization is shown in Figure 2.5.

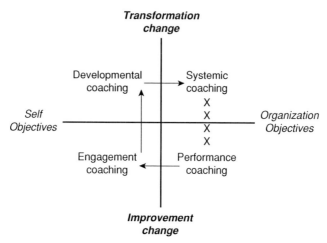

Figure 2.5   The route to organizational transformation

Coaching in the performance management corner, while important for improving individual performance, is unlikely to take the individual to transformation. Performance coaching imposes company objectives on employees for the benefit of the business. Performance coaching, within an organizational structure, while important for addressing corporate goals, is likely to lead to improvement, a laudable aim, but without changing the organization. Therefore this is unlikely to take the organization directly to systemic change shown by XXXX in the diagram.

When engagement coaching is introduced, employees are persuaded to voluntarily align their objectives with those of their employing organization. The objectives remain those of the organization and the changes are still limited to improvement.

The route to systemic change lies first through performance management, then to staff engagement with aligned objectives, then to development for individual transformation with individually owned objectives, and finally to organizational transformation, shown by ──➤ in Figure 2.5.

This route refers only to the development of employees which leads to organizational change. Many employees, who may not be aware of and therefore are assumed to lack interest in development, may well be pursuing individual development activities outside their work context. Tom Peters (Peters and Waterman 1982) noted this 30 years ago. For instance, Helena (a junior buyer in N&T) is a volunteer youth leader in her area and runs art group sessions for youngsters.

Transformation suggests that either employee or the organization (or both) will change. To achieve transformation, it is necessary to challenge the tfgs within the working environment, by, for example, testing a new policy on equal opportunities. For individual transformation, development coaching invites your client to identify the tfgs in which they work and consider its impact on them, as well as their contribution to it. For instance, John may reconsider his career prospect, and find the courage to go for a regional position, as the first black employee to do so in the company.

In a business, the systemic intent can be addressed by beginning with performance management, essential for efficiency, then engagement coaching as objectives are aligned, following through with one-to-one development coaching, where the aim is to enable the individual to work with their beliefs and feelings to transformation, and in the fullness of time become part of a larger changed system.

Systemic objectives

Systemic coaching programmes often aim to create a coaching culture in an organization. The organization aims to transform itself as a system through in-house performance and engagement coaching as well as development coaching by internal personnel or external practitioners. These programmes may also be supported by strategic team coaching.

> N&T are aiming to create a coaching culture and departmental managers have been put through short coaching training courses. These are designed to prepare middle managers to use coaching skills as part of their performance management. Coaching training also aims to improve the engagement of staff with N&T objectives. The HR director is piloting the provision of external coaches for particular individuals with a view to rolling out the support to all senior managers and board members.

For the organization to transform itself systemically, individual objectives and organization objectives must move towards each other, and ideally converge. Attempts to transform an organization directly through performance coaching are doomed to failure as the criteria for transformative change include ownership of objectives, access to emotions, an approach which creates powerful relationships.

> Jo, James and John are all three part of the coaching culture which this nationally recognized retail company is creating. The organization is using coaching to promote good practice, to improve performance, increase sales, develop staff and also to stimulate the changes needed to prosper in a competitive environment. This combination has the potential to transform the company.

Both performance and engagement aim for improved performance. There is evidence from Gallup research (2010) that an engaged workforce benefits the organization in financial, social and economic terms. Engaged employees are likely candidates for development and engagement coaching may move towards development in particular coaching relationships. Here we recommend that the contract is re-negotiated taking account of the new objectives of the coaching, the desired change and how the coaching is done.

Change through systemic coaching programmes

When Jo was promoted, 'coaching for line managers' was one of the first courses she attended. She was amazed to realize that empathy is part of coaching as well as questioning. On the course she learnt the LAW rule, meaning Listen And Wait for a feeling to be expressed. Then she learnt how to provide simple partial empathy, focusing only on the feelings which are relevant for performance. Her team leader Angela picked up Jo's empathic style and uses it with her team.

John receives external coaching from Catherine and she offers him advanced empathy about his fear of failure. The sessions are paid for out of part of the regional manager's budget dedicated to creating a coaching culture. He receives coaching with empathy from Catherine, and he begins to realize that change is not as rational as he had thought. His understanding of the role that emotions play in learning and change is exciting for him and he enrols on the Laura's next training for in-house coaching.

James offers Helen primary empathy and her commitment to the business was enhanced.

As HR manager, Laura suggests a week's leave for Helena and arranges for her to see an external counsellor who is retained by N&T for their staff. Laura hears about James' difficulties with his team and when Laura approaches James to confirm Helena's time off, she asks him how the team is performing. James admits to finding them a handful and she suggests coaching sessions for him with, Malcolm a highly-regarded executive coach. When James asks if the coach has retail experience, he is surprised to hear that the coach does not need to know all about the business as the coaching is not advice-giving but is about working on his own objectives. James' coaching sessions will be paid for from the clothing director's budget as part of the company's programme 'creating a coaching culture'.

Systemic coaching approach

How does an organization transform itself through creating a coaching culture? For systemic change, several initiatives will need to be in place:

- A robust performance management system is supported by managers using performance coaching.
- Engagement is stimulated by engagement coaching.

- Development coaching is offered to particular individuals often, but not always, in leadership roles.
- Senior teams are offered coaching.

When creating a coaching culture, Peter Hawkins recommends that the coaching should start with their leading operational staff and explains how this leads to transformation (Hawkins and Smith 2006). Thereafter, it is assumed that the change will cascade down the organization so this seems sensible. The concept of leadership is often associated with hierarchy as the leader is perceived to be powerful, superior and above others. He, and it is usually a man, is thought to have vision, drive and ambition. However, when the followers are asked in Gallup research polls what they value in a leader, none of these characteristics are mentioned. But trust is, and compassion, honesty and respect. Leaders who are empathic are likely to display these characteristics, unlike television leaders in *The Apprentice* and *Dragons' Den*. Empathy generates trust, compassion and respect in relationships and this applies at work as well as everywhere else. Marie Miyashiro's ground-breaking book, *The Empathy Factor*, identifies empathy as the missing element in leadership and organizational effectiveness. She reports that: 'Empathy is a valued currency – it allows us to create bonds of trust … insight into what others may be feeling or thinking … and informs our decisions.' She also states: 'Effective leaders seem better at blending the softer leadership skills – trust, empathy and genuine communication – with the tough skills needed to keep an organization afloat during difficult times' (Miyashiro 2011: 24).

For systemic change in an organization the powerful and responsible members must be prepared to change both themselves and the systems in it. For example training managers to coach with partial empathy will result in good performance management which does not stress overworked line managers. Engagement coaching with primary empathy by senior managers will move the organization towards development for key employees. Development coaching with primary and advanced empathy, for those in responsible roles will enable the system changes needed for organizational transformation.

Summary

In this chapter we have presented three contexts for different types of coaching which may be part of the fourth, the route to systemic organizational transformation. Performance and engagement coaching, including partial and primary empathy, are needed for corporate and business success. However, for organizational transformation, there must be development coaching where individuals are offered coaching opportunities to make changes in their personal and professional life. Empathy acts as a trigger to change which will be in direct proportion to the level of empathy offered to your client.

Partial empathy is right for performance coaching, primary empathy supports engagement coaching, while advanced empathy supports development for transformation. For systemic coaching, the organization itself may develop an empathic style, where it listens to and understands its stakeholders. Systemic coaching programmes aim to promote the transformation of a company, an organization, or an institution within society. The aim is to transform the organization through complete re-structuring or culture change programmes. In many such programmes, change is sought through rational argument and persuasion. In the following chapters we explain why this rational approach is doomed to failure, as many are.

3   Neuroscience and empathy

In this chapter we present a summary of the neuroscientific evidence for empathy and attachment patterns. We complete the chapter with a tour of defence mechanisms and a brief summary of the Drama Triangle.

Neuroscience is the empirical study of the brain and connected nervous system. Both nature and nurture affect the brain as it develops – the brain changes constantly as a result of learning and remains 'plastic' throughout life. However, the Royal Society report, *Brain Waves*, published in 2011, warns against 'overemphasizing the role of the brain at the expense of a holistic understanding of cultural life based on interpretation and empathy'.

Throughout this book we emphasize that empathy is a skill that enhances your ability to coach clients; that the skill is necessary to enable a client to achieve their aims. Empathy applies whether the coaching is for performance, engagement or development. Being able to empathize means being able to understand accurately the other person's position, to identify with 'where they are at'. In doing so, the other person feels valued, as their thoughts and feelings have been heard, acknowledged and respected. Empathy supports your client as they address potential change.

Simon Baron-Cohen, a neuroscientist, has explored the spectrum of empathy through measurement of brain activity in his book, *Zero Degrees of Empathy*, published in 2011. He reports findings from those showing little or no empathy to those who are able to use the skill with remarkable effect. His data results in the familiar bell-shaped curve showing empathy ranging from zero to high empathy. The range is determined by the empathizing mechanism in the brain which indicates how you empathize with your client. In an attempt to measure empathy, Baron-Cohen created the Empathy Quotient questionnaire.

The Empathy Quotient questionnaire devised by Simon Baron-Cohen includes statements which describe empathic behaviour:

1. I find it easy to put myself in somebody else's shoes.
2. I can usually appreciate the other person's viewpoint even if I don't agree with it.

3. I am quick to spot when someone is feeling awkward or uncomfortable.
4. I am good at understanding how others are feeling.
5. Friends usually talk to me about their problems as they say I am very understanding.
6. I can easily tell if someone is interested in what I am saying.
7. I can tune into how someone feels rapidly and intuitively.
8. I can easily work out what another person might want to talk about.
9. I can pick up quickly if someone says one thing but means another.
10. I can tell if someone is masking their true emotion.

And non-empathic behaviour:

1. I find it difficult to explain to others things that I understand easily, when they don't understand it first time.
2. People often tell me that I went too far in driving my point home in discussion.
3. It is hard for me to see why some things upset people so much.
4. Seeing people cry doesn't really upset me.
5. If I say something that someone else is offended by, I think that that's their problem not mine.
6. I am very blunt, which some people take to be rudeness, even though this is unintentional.
7. I can't always see why someone should have been offended by a remark.
8. I am able to make decisions without being influenced by people's feelings.
9. Other people often say that I am insensitive, though I don't always see why.

If the items in the second list remind you of the captains of industry who grace our television screens, you will see why organizations talk about empathy but often don't put it into practice. This zero empathy may be rewarded by promotion and even knighthoods.

The entire questionnaire can be found in the book, *Zero Degrees of Empathy.*

Recently scientists, more specifically neuroscientists, have examined how our emotions, including empathy, have a basis in the functioning of our brain. Indeed, much of this knowledge is thanks to functional magnetic resonance imaging for giving a clear picture of the brain areas that play a central role when we empathize.

Discoveries in neuroscience

Penfield with the probe

Dr Wilder Penfield carried out research in the 1950s when ethics committees were not as powerful as they are now. He was allowed to stimulate the brain of his patients with electronic probes while they were conscious (no pain is involved in brain stimulation). His probes touched certain parts of the brain and the person 'remembered' their feelings about specific events in their past. His results provided some of the evidence used by Eric Berne to develop the system used in coaching and management development known as Transactional Analysis (TA). His very informative book, *Games People Play*, published originally in 1964, included life games, marital games, party games, sexual games and many others. The TA system recognizes that humans retain messages from their earliest experiences which influence their behaviour as adults.

This rather crude method of examining the brain in the 1950s was dramatically improved in the 1970s through the use of brain scanning techniques which produce multiple images of the brain, so that it can be viewed in detail while the patient is lying inside the CT or fMRI scanner. (CT stands for Computerized Tomography and fMRI stands for functional Magnetic Resonance Imaging.) Scanning identifies areas of changing blood flows in the brain associated with neural activity. This method is being improved all the time and new techniques are becoming available.

Three brains

The results of brain scanning gave a much fuller understanding of what is going on in our heads, which have evolved over millions of years. Scanning confirmed some of the details about the brain which had only been guessed at by scientists. A simplified diagram of the brain is shown in Figure 3.1.

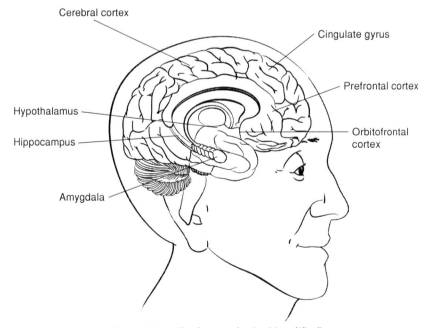

Figure 3.1   The human brain (simplified)

The earliest area of the brain to develop is the brain stem (which consists of the midbrain, pons and medulla oblongata), and this is used to test whether a person in a coma is medically dead. If there is no response from the brain stem, the patient is certified as dead. This early brain persists in fighting for your life – doing its best to keep the automatic systems of the body going, like breathing, heart rate, etc. Your brain stem is in direct contact with your body and the other parts of your brain, sending messages in each direction.

The second brain to develop, known as the limbic system, wrapped around the early brain, forms part of the inner border with the cortex which is the outermost layer of the brain. Limbic means border. The limbic system belongs to the mammal stage of evolution and is important for emotions, memory and relationships. A frog or a goldfish doesn't have much of a relationship with you but your dog or cat does because their functioning is more developed. The limbic system, developed early in life, has three parts: the amygdala, the hypothalamus and the hippocampus. Some sources also include the thalamus.

The amygdala (pronounced am-ig-dalla) is the almond-shaped cluster of cells which can both receive and send emotional signals. Every human has two of these important organs for managing relationships located just behind each ear. If you draw an imaginary line straight through the front of your eye and one through your ear, where the lines would cross would be where the amygdala is. They support a variety of functions including emotion, behaviour and long-term memory. Your amygdalae react to situations that are fearful or uncertain by firing off chemical messages in various directions, including impulses to the hypothalamus.

The hypothalamus (hi-po-thal-a-moss) provides a system to deal with stress through sending messages to glands in the body which generate hormones. When you are afraid or stressed, your hypothalamus sends nerve impulse to produce adrenalin, a very necessary reaction to danger. The complicated neurochemistry results in a rise in cortisol levels, and this can be measured easily in your saliva, when you are excited, scared or stressed. This is known as the stress response. At times of danger, the stress response makes sure that you survive through its fight or flight (or sometimes even freeze) instructions. When the body is overloaded with cortisol, in persistent stress situations, the effect is described as 'corrosive' because too much has a damaging effect on the body, compromising the immune system, appetite and sleep patterns. Worse than this, is the effect that persistently high cortisol levels may have on the hippocampus, the regulator of hormone levels.

The hippocampus is a sensitive part of the brain, developing early in life together with the amygdala in response to experience of love and care. Romanian orphans were found to have less developed amygdalae, hippocampi and parts of their cortex. The hippocampus can be damaged by too much cortisol and stops doing its task of monitoring hormone levels. When this occurs, the hippocampus fails to inform the hypothalamus that there is enough cortisol. The hypothalamus in turn fails to use its 'off' switch and the stress response goes on and on. The hippocampus plays an important role in memory, and in Alzheimer's disease is one of the first areas to suffer damage. When the hippocampus is damaged, the link to the third brain is affected and leads to severe cognitive deficits.

The third brain is the cerebral cortex which wraps right round the limbic system and also develops in response to social interaction. The cortex developed with primates and became a fully human brain with the development of a pre-frontal cortex, which is just behind your forehead. Only mammals have this brain and it allows you to reflect, think in abstractions and connect through neurons to the other two parts of your brain. So your pre-frontal cortex makes sense of everything else that the brain knows or has ever known. This is where mirror neurons fire when you offer your client an empathic response. They are called mirror neurons because they fire when the person reports particular feelings. The orbito-frontal cortex, which is nearest to your amygdala just behind your eyes, ensures that you can relate to others sensitively and is considered important for empathy. In a shocking study, Romanian orphans who were cut off from close contact with a carer, kept in cots all day, unable to make relationships, had a virtual black hole where their orbitofrontal cortex should be (Chugani et al. 2001).

Each section of the brain is powerful in its own way, and serves to protect you from harm. The fight or flight reaction instructs the emotional brain above to release adrenalin to give your limbs energy. The emotional brain evaluates what you meet in life, drawing on memory and feelings, so you don't accept sweets from strangers, and passes on the message to the motor centre of your brain to make you run away. The pre-frontal cortex helps you to learn, identify a safer route home, and maybe decide to go with a friend next time. The orbito-frontal cortex ensures that you are able to express emotion honestly and respond to it in others with empathy.

The three brains can be thought of as the basic tool shed at the base of the brain, above which the emotional systems develop, and beyond them both lies the pre-frontal cortex and cingulate, where emotional experience is processed and alternative courses of action considered.

The EMPATHY CIRCUIT: a summary

Imaging shows that the empathy circuit consists of at least ten regions of the brain. First, the pre-frontal cortex compares your own perspective with anothers' and considers others' thoughts and feelings. The orbito-frontal cortex is up next to judge the emotional charge and react to it. The language centre in the empathy circuit ensures that you can speak about emotion; the gyrus and cingulate areas enable you to perceive another's emotional state. Further sections of the cerebral cortex check out your own awareness, make estimates of others' emotions or intentions, monitor gaze, and react to touch. There are neurons (known as mirror neurons) which fire when you are doing the same thing as someone else, mimicking or following someone's gaze. The jewel in the crown of the empathy circuit is the amygdala, where emotional learning is thought to take place, as highly charged and arousing experiences are registered there. The neuroscientist Joseph Le Doux, considered to be the amygdala expert, established the importance of eye contact as the eyes give clues to emotion. He was so keen on the amygdala that he formed a band called *The Amygdaloids*. When psychopathic brains are scanned, abnormalities in the empathy circuit are revealed with the amygdala being particularly affected.

A brain in two halves

Although a brain looks like a football it is actually in two halves, a right hemisphere (Greek, meaning half a sphere) and a left hemisphere. An understanding of their different roles is important for those who have been educated to believe that logic and rationality are the answers to everything. The right hemisphere develops early when the infant has no words but lots of feelings, and children draw and sing before they can talk. Sue Gerhardt in her lovely book, *Why Love Matters* (2004), presents evidence that the right orbito-frontal cortex is larger than the left and children build this part of their brain through being loved. Gerhardt describes the power of a smile from mother or father as actually helping the brain to grow its emotional muscle. This is why you can detect emotion in the facial expression of your client. The left hemisphere develops later and concentrates on language and logic so very much needed even to understand this sentence. You can sense how developed your two halves are by doing the following exercise:

> Lie down and relax. Starting with your right side, identify each part of your body in turn starting with your right toe and working your way up gradually to the top of your head. Note the sensations in each part of your body. The process directs your left brain attention to distant areas of your awareness. Now repeat the process on the left side of your body. There may be a slight difference. Next try to connect to the sensations in your inner organs (thought to be attended to by the right hemisphere). If this is difficult, your right hemisphere may not be as developed as your left. The exercise itself is known to develop the ability, so trying to identify where in your body a feeling is 'felt' is another way to train the right hemisphere.

How do these three brains and two sides apply to coaching with empathy?

As mentioned above, a significant area of the brain relating to our emotions is the amygdala. The amygdala stores the brain's alarm system in the event of acute stress and jumps into action when threatened. This means that when a person faces a dangerous or difficult situation, the amygdala is activated.

The amygdala learns from day one so childhood events influence it, holding the memory for ever.

David

David was born to military parents, who travelled the world as part of their role in the British army, and David was cared for by different servants in every country. When he was five years old, David was sent to boarding school in England, missed his mother dreadfully, and was bullied and ridiculed for his tearfulness. When his parents visited, David tried to tell them but they wanted to jolly him out of it and couldn't understand his dread of them leaving again. David's amygdala learnt that sudden change was painful and threatened his well-being. His Top Secret File holds the memory for ever.

Because the abandonment may happen in very early in childhood, the effect is powerful, threatening and negative. The conscious memory of this traumatic event will be forgotten but remains in the unconscious memory of the amygdala. David's reaction to change will include the memory. Many children brought up in the developed world have experienced the absence of their mother or carer because of illness, although this is less likely now as hospital practice has moved on in this regard. Other cultures may reduce the effect of mother-separation by their extended family, where grandmother or aunt would become a temporary carer.

What happens when the amygdala is activated?

The memory of such an event may be stimulated in later life when similar events occur, like being 'dumped' by a partner, or losing a job. Almost any change can trigger the amygdala which is super-sensitive. Only the pre-frontal cortex can override the amygdala, and too much cortisol may affect its ability to do this. Even the threat of such events may cause the individual to close down temporarily, unwilling to face the change in life that may be happening, so that flight, fight or freeze results in the person when faced with a dangerous or difficult situation.

Accessing the amygdala's memories of both threats and happy times can support coaching. For instance, a person may be fearful of giving presentations.

Brian

Although a successful director, Brian (introduced in Chapter 1) is terrified of giving presentations. When Martina says: 'Tell me about your presentation', he says: 'It's awful, I just dry and die' and immediately he feels sick and sweaty. Martina can see his pallor and sweat. She says: 'You look really pale and frightened.' Brian explains that he actually experiences terror and feels frozen. He says he has attended presentation training with no improvement.

As a good coach, Martina gets Brian to be more specific and describe his last presentation. He says the feelings are so bad that before the event he can't eat or sleep.

When he tells her about the actual event, he appears excited and gives her a convincing mini-presentation. She responds to his expressions of enthusiasm, saying: 'You really feel passionate about this, don't you?' When they unpack what is different, he says it's the audience and the exposure that frighten him and it's worse than school. On enquiry, school included events where Brian experienced the shame of being 'shown up' as not good enough in front of the others in his class. He always felt rather second-rate and still does in this situation even though he has a successful career. Brian's presentations are almost always to an audience of his peers and he can soon feel like the little boy at school, stumbling over his words and unsure of himself.

Martina asks him to imagine how his peers are feeling and he describes them as unaware of what he has to offer so they are interested, otherwise they wouldn't be there. He also realizes that most of them are not strangers but know him as a competent and inspiring director. Martina works with Brian to expand his range of feelings around presentations. These are likely to include excitement, confidence and hope, and they agree on a plan for a practice run with his own team.

Martina did not avoid the negative feelings Brian was experiencing and identified the origin of them in his Top Secret File. She also responded empathically to his excitement and enthusiasm about his presentation, giving him a model to emulate for himself. Visioning is used here to take Brian into a future event armed with strong feelings and resourceful attitude.

Attachment and a secure base

Early childhood experience can affect how adults relate to others, particularly through their attachment patterns. These were first identified by child psychologists, John Bowlby and Mary Ainsworth, based on their observations of children with their mother or carer and a stranger (Ainsworth et al. 1978).The 'strange-situation' research has been replicated many times (mother means mother or carer) since then, and the results are as follows:

- *Secure attachment*: the child explores without anxiety, notes the departure of mother, cries briefly, is easily distracted by play (without engaging the stranger) and welcomes her return. This pattern is known as a 'secure base' as it allows for exploration and development as well as safety. According to some psychological researchers, a child becomes securely attached when the mother is available and able to meet the needs of the child in a responsive and appropriate manner. The length of contact time with mother is not relevant.
- *Insecure attachment. Ambivalent*: Here the child is too anxious and clingy to explore and is wary of strangers, even when the mother is present. When the mother departs, the child is extremely distressed.

The child will be ambivalent when she returns – wanting to be close to the mother but resentful, and also resistant when she tries to pick him up. According to some psychological researchers, this style develops from a mothering style which is engaged but unpredictable. That is, sometimes the child's needs are ignored until some other activity is completed, and that attention is sometimes given to the child more through the needs of the parent than from the child's initiation.

- *Insecure attachment. Avoidant*: here the child will avoid or ignore the mother – showing little emotion when the mother departs or returns. The child may run away from the mother when she approaches and fail to cling to her when picked up. The child will not explore very much regardless of who is there. Strangers will not be treated much differently from the mother. There is not much emotional range regardless of who is in the room or if it is empty. This pattern of attachment develops from a care-giving style which is more disengaged. The child's needs are frequently not met and the child comes to believe that communication of his feelings and needs has no influence on the caregiver.
- A further category known as *disorganized attachment* appears in children who have been neglected or abused.

How do these patterns affect your adult clients?

Ambivalent insecure attachment can be recognized in Jason (the accountant introduced in Chapter 1) who had a rather protected childhood.

Jason's mother tended to be over-anxious and, in the absence of his father, struggled to provide for her child. She ensured his safety by limiting risk and her attention was intermittent as a consequence of having to earn a living. Jason experienced his mother as unpredictable because of her commitments. She was available one minute and preoccupied the next and Jason's pattern of attachment is insecure/ambivalent. This is a not unusual childhood experience, shared by millions of people. Jason developed into a rather serious youngster. As an adult, Jason keeps his distance in relationships in his personal life as well as his work life. He has chosen a career which minimizes his contact with clients and when he is given responsibility for a team of young trainee accountants, finds them flippant and casual, in contrast to his serious and reserved style. We discuss how Jason finds a secure base through empathy in Chapter 6.

Avoidant insecure attachment can be recognized in John (the N&T store manager introduced in Chapter 2).

John was brought up in a working-class area as part of a large family with both parents working. He was given strong values of responsibility and honesty from both parents and plenty of experience as the eldest in the family.

His early contact with his mother was limited by the demands of the other children and her work. He learnt to look after himself at an early age. He was not encouraged to express his opinions or his feelings and he learnt to 'forget' them. John did well at school and joined N&T straight from school. As a good employee, John was promoted quickly and his current role is general manager of a large retail store. He finds real difficulty in relating to any difficulties his staff may experience, being emotionally distant, and only attends to them when mistakes have been made. His staff describe him as cold (a sign of insecure attachment) although he appears confident (not always a sign of secure attachment). He remains single, as he says he has no time for dating. We discuss in Chapter 6 how John finds a secure base through empathy.

Secure attachment can be recognized in James (the N&T buyer introduced in Chapter 2).

James has experienced consistent mothering as his family were comfortable with a successful business in tailoring and his mother did not work. Although not a perfect mother, she was available to her sons and encouraged them to be adventurous and explore. James is well educated and confident in himself, although somewhat reserved (not necessarily a sign of insecure attachment). James is keen to learn and develop, being open to change, and excited by his work. James is lucky to have a secure base as part of his life experience.

Disorganized attachment can be recognized in Ron, a middle manager.

Ron was brought up by very strict parents. In fact, his father was aggressive and beat him as a child 'for his own good', especially if his school report was not good enough. He would hide in a cupboard to avoid his violence. Ron developed a tough persona and a thuggish exterior which hid his true hurt and deeply lonely feelings. As an adult, he is pushy, insulting and aggressive, particularly to women colleagues. The company need to deal with his behaviour or risk a bullying complaint.

As these feelings are likely to be in his locked trunk, Ron should be referred for counselling or therapy (see Chapter 8).

Defence mechanisms

It is important to realize that defence mechanisms are life-preserving and therefore part of a healthy and natural human existence. However, defence mechanisms may be getting in the way of learning for your client. The idea of a part of each person which is unconscious and inaccessible may not be something you will discuss with your clients, nor need you. The unconscious works for your client to maintain an image of self which they find acceptable. The unconscious uses defence mechanisms to keep the self-image in place, and plays its part in maintaining the psychological health of every individual. The Freudian basis of defence mechanisms is challenged by some practitioners but the idea of an active unconscious has become accepted in most helping professions.

Defensive behaviours are usually caused by a current event which triggers anxiety with its roots in the past. Anxiety may take the form of 'self-talk' like: 'Will I be accepted/wanted/liked? Will I understand what's going on? Will I be able to do what's required?' These messages are the echo of past distress and come from the fear of being rejected or overwhelmed. They are real for anyone and you cannot see your own defence mechanisms because they are unconscious.

Defence mechanisms include:

- *Atonement*: Making up for a previous fault by performing a socially approved act, e.g. a member of staff staying late to make up for being lazy during the day.
- *Compensation*: Anxiety in one area is balanced by achievement in another, e.g. failure to achieve promotion can be compensated for by excessive sociability or obsessive domesticity.
- *Denial*: Protection from painful reality by refusing to recognize it, e.g. your client believing they're doing OK at work when they are due for a report or final warning.
- *Displacement*: Transfer of feelings or actions to another person to reduce anxiety, e.g. if your client is angry with someone at work, they may displace it to you.
- *Fantasy*: Creating an imaginary world to meet a desired goal, e.g. your client's belief that things are better than they are.
- *Identification*: Trying to 'become' an admired person by imitating dress and language. Your client may begin to adopt sayings or gestures of yours.
- *Intellectualization*: Masking anxious feelings by intellectual and detached discussion, e.g. discussion of strategy when staff are leaving in droves.
- *Introjection*: Adoption of someone else's beliefs or attitudes, e.g. your client believes they are no good because a powerful parent said so.
- *Projection*: Sending undesirable feelings on to someone else, e.g. your client acting as if another member of staff is angry when it's they who are angry.
- *Transference*: A particular kind of projection where your client projects on to you aspects of their historical relationship with parents, e.g. adoration or rebellion.
- *Rationalization*: A client creating rational but unreal reasons for their own behaviour, e.g. staff who blame management for their own lack of motivation.

- *Reaction formation*: Disguising real feelings or attitudes by the opposite behaviour, e.g. your client expressing disgust about someone's behaviour but enjoying gossiping about it.
- *Regression*: This is reversion to an earlier stage of development, e.g. your client having a temper tantrum or sleeping a lot under stress.
- *Repression*: Unconscious exclusion of past memories and feelings to prevent pain anxiety or guilt, e.g. someone who forgets they have been abused. These are the contents of your client's locked trunk described in Chapter 1.
- *Suppression*: Conscious exclusion of past memories and feelings to prevent pain, anxiety and guilt, e.g. the client who 'forgets' he or she was bullied at school. These are the contents of your client's Top Secret File described in Chapter 1.

As a coach, your role does not include trying to reveal your client's unconscious defence mechanisms, but a skilled coach will take account of them, particularly the phenomenon of projection and transference.

How can you spot defence mechanisms?

Freudian slips are clues to the existence of defence mechanisms. For example, someone denying anger about a colleague's promotion may say: 'I'm so pleased I could hit him' (denial). Other clues to defence mechanisms are non-verbal behaviour such as false smiles, twitching limbs or a sarcastic tone of voice. When clients' statements are exaggerations or generalizations, there is likely to be a defence mechanism lurking. If clients tend to talk about others rather than themselves, this may be another clue. e.g. 'the team are not happy with our new project' may be an example of displacement, fantasy or projection.

The feelings that are most likely to be hidden by defence mechanisms are shame, anger, anxiety and hurt, and although the trigger is in the present, the feelings are hidden in the past. Some of them (in your client's Top Secret File) are susceptible to coaching whereas others (in their locked trunk) are best referred to a therapist. To bring these deeper feelings into their conscious mind, your client would need to feel very safe and referral is advised. We identify some below.

Projection

Your client may 'project' their own feelings onto others, especially if they are uncomfortable feelings like anger or sadness. This means that your client sends out the feeling to someone else so that they don't have to feel it.

> The person defends against threatening and unacceptable feelings and impulses by acting as though these feelings and impulses only exist in other people, not in the person himself or herself.
>
> (McLeod 1998: 43)

For instance, your client Angela may not be comfortable with expressing anger (it being hidden in her Top Secret File), so unconsciously sends the feeling out to her colleague Barbara, who then expresses it for them. What happens to Barbara in this situation?

When Barbara finds herself feeling angry about something, while Angela remains as cool as a cucumber, this may be projection. When the projected feeling is 'taken in' by Barbara, she kind of swallows what has been sent unconsciously to her, it becomes part of her, and this is called projective identification.

Projective identification

Projective identification is an unconscious transaction between two people, i.e. between what one person feels and what the other feels.

Angela

Angela has been landed with extra work in order to release one of her staff. In a management briefing she is speaking calmly and without apparent emotion, projecting some feelings of anger about her boss, onto her colleague and close friend, Barbara. Angela has unconsciously learned that angry feelings are unacceptable to have and she pushes them away from herself by unconsciously 'seeing' them in others. This means that she is not conscious that her anger is really part of her own self, having learnt in the past, that being 'good' was being 'not angry'.

Barbara, quite unconsciously, takes in the feeling of anger projected at her, experiences it as real, and may feel impelled to express anger about the extra work. Hence what Barbara is feeling in that moment, is really part of Angela, but appears to both Angela and Barbara as part of Barbara.

Projective identification occurs when the person to whom the feelings and impulses are being projected is manipulated into believing that he or she actually has these feelings and impulses (McLeod 1998: 43), e.g. Barbara feeling angry above or the CEO believing he is invincible.

What is the benefit for Angela projecting anger onto Barbara and for Barbara to express it?

Angela can allow herself to disapprove of Barbara's anger, and may react strongly to Barbara. The clue to projection is the strength of feeling which Angela may now have about the part of herself she perceives in Barbara, as theory suggests that this is how she really feels about her angry self but defends against this knowledge by projection. This is why taking back projections is incredibly illuminating. The perceived aspect of Barbara, being angry, which Angela reacts too strongly, suggests that anger is something which clearly has importance for Angela. This is why projection has been called a gift in the present from the past as the clue to your self lies in your reaction to the other. In coaching, her strength of feeling will betray Angela's projection, and a skilled coach may work with Angela's feelings about the extra work she has been given. Barbara may also recognize through coaching that her feelings of anger are not her own but projective identification.

Coaches must not underestimate the fearful nature of some projective material – it is being sent out to another in order to lessen the pain or fear which your client would experience if they 'owned' it properly. Hence, where projection may be identified in coaching, great care is needed. As a skilled coach you can help your clients to unlock these defences, usually by making possible projections implicit, e.g. by noting that Angela is feeling angry about her treatment at work but it's someone else who is angry about it. Angela can be invited to explore why this is occurring and what might change for her if she were to be angry for herself.

Transference

Another form of projection is the defence known as *transference*. Where feelings experienced in the past are 'transferred' unconsciously into present relationships, the term transference is used. These feelings are not just memories, they are alive and can deeply affect current relationships. Transference is thought to repeat the love, aggression or frustration experienced as a child in relation to his parents. In addition, they may not be all negative, and can take the form of undiluted admiration *or* hostility. The emotions and feelings involved are repetitions of the original ones.

Transference can be seen as an entirely normal occurrence in any relationship and may have childhood contents, i.e. the idealized father or perfect mother. If this seems a fanciful idea, the idea of transference has been applied to everyday living by Robert de Board in his highly entertaining *Counselling for Toads* (1997). In the story of Toad going for counselling, Toad may be transferring his own feelings onto Badger and Heron. For instance, when a client humbly and deferentially asks their coach for the benefit of their advice, based on their extensive experience, they may have 'transferred' feelings of undue deference onto their coach. On the other hand, the transferred feelings may be resentment or hostility especially in performance coaching.

Counter-transference

This is an unconscious response to transference. As a coach, you are typecast or propelled into the matching pre-prepared script, and may experience counter-transference. Although not everyone agrees with it, the idea is that emotions are felt to match with the projected transferred feelings. The client's over-deference as above, may give rise to corresponding god-like and all-powerful feelings in you. Resentment may trigger an impatience with the 'childish behaviour' of the client. Where clients display feelings of resentment or anger, from the hurt child within, then you need to resist the temptation to offer a punishing response. Similarly you may need to resist being carried away by the undiluted admiration given by some clients, and, alternatively perhaps, dare to reveal the cracks!

In the case of transference and counter-transference, the task for you as coach is to disentangle what may be your own feelings from what is being unconsciously transferred to you by your client. For instance, where you feel an urge to rescue your client – surely not an appropriate feeling between adults, this may alert you to the possibility that the feeling is counter-transference. You are feeling the urge to rescue in response to your client's feelings of helplessness, and this may also be happening to your client's colleagues as well. You may choose to mention your 'rescue' feeling and discuss whether it is appropriate to your client's situation.

These ideas offer useful information in the service of your client and material for advanced empathy.

How might you respond with empathy to the other defence mechanisms mentioned above?

- *Atonement*: Making up for previous faults by performing a socially approved act, e.g. a member of staff staying late to make up for being lazy during the day.

(Repetition and advanced empathy: perhaps you feel satisfied because your overtime has made up for slacking earlier.)

- *Compensation*: Anxiety in one area is balanced by achievement in another, e.g. failure to achieve promotion can be compensated for by excessive partying.

(Advanced empathy: I guess you felt justified in having a blow out – you seemed disappointed.)

- *Denial*: Protection from painful reality by refusing to recognize it, e.g. your client believing they're doing OK at work when they are due for a report or final warning.

(Advanced empathy + challenge: you seem sure that your appraisal will be OK … I'm wondering about that warning you mentioned earlier.)

- *Displacement*: Transfer of feelings or actions to another person to reduce anxiety, e.g. if your client is angry with someone at work, he or she may displace it onto you.

(Advanced empathy as challenge: you seem cross with me this evening.)

- *Fantasy*: Creating an imaginary world to meet a desired goal, e.g. your client's belief that things are better than they are.

(Advanced empathy + confrontation: you seem excited and this sounds great – I'd be interested to hear the details.)

- *Identification*: Trying to 'become' the admired person by imitating dress and language. Your client may begin to adopt sayings or gestures of yours.

(Challenge: I notice we're wearing the same colours again today.)

- *Intellectualization*: Masking anxious feelings by intellectual and detached discussion, e.g. your client discussing strategy when staff are leaving in droves.

(Advanced empathy: you must be worried about the retention rates.)

- *Introjection*: Adoption of someone else's beliefs or attitudes, e.g. your client believes he or she is no good because a powerful parent said so.

(Advanced empathy: you sound convinced about this – can you tell me more?)

- *Projection*: Sending undesirable feelings on to someone else, e.g. your client acting as if another member of staff is angry when it's they who are angry.

(Advanced empathy as challenge: you must be miffed to be given extra work.)

- *Transference*: A particular kind of projection where your client projects on to you aspects of his or her historical relationship with parents or carers, e.g. adoration or rebellion.

(Advanced empathy as challenge: you seem unhappy about being here.)

- *Rationalization*: Your client creating rational but unreal reasons for their own behaviour, e.g. staff who blame management for their own lack of motivation.

(Advanced empathy as confrontation: you don't sound entirely happy about this yourself.)

- *Reaction formation*: Disguising real feelings or attitudes by the opposite behaviour, e.g. your client expressing disgust about someone's behaviour but enjoying gossiping about it.

(Advanced empathy as confrontation: actually you sound rather pleased about her behaviour.)

- *Regression*: This is reversion to an earlier stage of development, e.g. your client having a temper tantrum or sleeping a lot under stress.

(Referral, see Chapter 8.)

- *Repression*: Unconscious exclusion of past memories and feelings to prevent pain anxiety or guilt, e.g. someone who forgets they have been abused. These are the contents of your client's locked trunk described in Chapter 1.

(Referral, see Chapter 8.)

- *Suppression*: Conscious exclusion of past memories and feelings to prevent pain, anxiety and guilt, e.g. the person who 'forgets' he or she was bullied at school. These are the contents of your client's Top Secret File described in Chapter 1.

(Advanced empathy as confrontation: you seem vague about your own school experience.)

Sometimes in work relationships, several defence mechanisms can be in play together and they support each other as people collude with each other. A useful model for dealing with collusive defence mechanisms is the drama triangle.

The Drama Triangle

This summary is based on the work of Stephen Karpman (2006). The Drama Triangle is an unconscious game which can appear in human relations everywhere. As mentioned above, Eric Berne developed the concept of games and how they are played in everyday life. For coaches it is most likely to appear in work relationships. The game involves at least three players and anyone can find themselves playing it. The simple, three-player version of the game is illustrated in Figure 3.2.

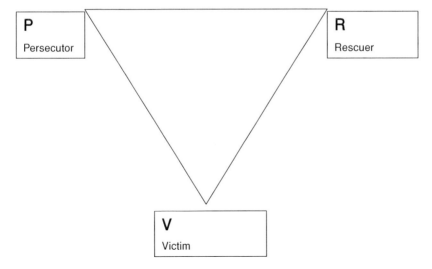

Figure 3.2   The Drama Triangle

The Drama Triangle consists of three players; the Persecutor, the Rescuer and the Victim. The roles rarely exist in healthy relationships or lead to effective performance. The roles are described below.

The Rescuer

The Rescuer is uncomfortable with another's anxiety and often offers rescue without being asked. They are most comfortable when 'saving' the Victim from an attack by the Persecutor with the assumption that the Victim is unable to solve their own issues. The pay-off for the Rescuer is feeling superior to the Victim. By constantly rescuing others, they can also avoid dealing with their own problems and issues. There is often collusion between the Victim and the Rescuer, which allows them to join forces against the bullying tactics of the Persecutor. The Rescuer does more than their share in emotional care, thinking and problem-solving.

This process only exists as long as both parties remain in their dramatic positions. As part of the game, players can 'switch' at any time to another role. The Rescuer may feel hurt when they are blamed for unfortunate outcomes and may switch into Victim role.

The Victim

The Victim's role in the Drama Triangle is based on the pretext that they are unable to take care of themselves. This stance is often the result of learned helplessness in childhood. The Victim feels powerless, hopeless, depressed and oppressed. The Victim learns to find people to rescue them, i.e. to make decisions for them and to defend against Persecutors. The pay-off for this position is that the Victim avoids making decisions and avoids having to learn the problem-solving skills necessary to manage independently of the Rescuer. The person on the receiving end of the Persecutor's actions often feels overtly threatened and uneasy and may over-react to challenge. The Victim can easily switch to Persecutor if the Rescuer lets them down.

The Persecutor

The Persecutor role is likely to be blaming, critical, judgemental and overtly controlling. They do not believe that the victim can solve problems for themselves and tends to dismiss the Victim's efforts. The Persecutor often comes across as rigid and authoritarian and is driven by a sense of being right. Their focus is more task-driven than relationship-driven and they may force their solution on the Victim. When things go wrong and they are held responsible, they can switch to Victim role.

How does the Drama Triangle appear in the workplace?

Angela and Barbara (mentioned above) are a good example. Angela at this point is in Victim mode, talking about the extra work she has been given and telling Barbara all about it. She gives the impression of being helpless to do anything about the situation and Barbara becomes increasingly angry on behalf of Angela although Barbara is not involved in the situation at all. The Prosecutor is their manager Graham, who has allocated the extra work to Angela without consulting her as he is used to her passive acceptance in the past. Angela and Barbara collude in their criticism of Graham, Barbara accepts Angela's version as the truth, believes her unable to deal with it herself, and takes on responsibility by confronting Graham. He, as Persecutor, is convinced he is right, repeats his opinion rather aggressively, and triggers a union meeting.

Thereafter, Graham takes the Victim role while Angela remains in Victim role while Barbara leads her colleagues in Persecutor role. In the fullness of time, when Angela loses her bonus, she blames Barbara who then switches into Victim role to match Angela's Persecutor role. The dance can continue indefinitely.

You may like to identify the defence mechanisms at work here.

The Antidote Triangle

The way out of the Drama Triangle is presented by the Antidote Triangle, which is represented in Figure 3.3.

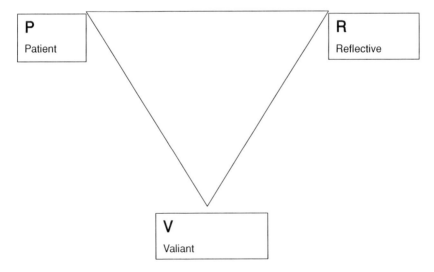

Figure 3.3 The Antidote Triangle

The Antidote Triangle presents an alternative to the Drama Triangle. The players choose to respond to the event with respectful enquiry and empathy.

This version also needs each player to establish clear boundaries and learn to relate to others assertively. Coaching can help each player to make the necessary changes. In order to achieve freedom from the Drama Triangle, the individual players need to make the following changes:

The Rescuer becomes Reflective

The Rescuer reflects on their need to nurture others at their own expense. The Rescuer will establish what feelings are their own and which are projected from others. They may reflect that they tend to over-react in conflict situations which are not their own. Giving up the need to feel superior to the Victim can result in the Rescuer learning to take better care of their own needs directly and honestly.

The Victim becomes Valiant

The Victim needs to recognize their part in being victimized and what they gain from maintaining this role. They must be prepared to be powerful and assert themselves in conflict situations. They may need to dare to be open about what they are feeling, and this is part of skilled assertive communication. By becoming more assertive and learning the skills necessary to manage on their own, the Victim can become independent and self-sufficient.

The Persecutor becomes Patient

The Persecutor is becomes patient and allows the other two players to express their feelings while they listen. The Persecutor tolerates conflict as a learning opportunity. In addition, the Persecutor needs to be willing to give up the pay-off gained in the form of feeling superior and powerful over others. The Persecutor can then experience more equal and authentic interactions with others.

You may like to consider how our trio above use the Antidote Triangle and change the ending?

Summary

In this chapter we have summarized the information from neuroscientists about emotions and empathy. Scanning technology has identified several parts of the brain which become active when people feel emotions or offer empathy. Depending on the nature of the feeling the brain issues instructions to its neighbouring parts. When a client is facing change or choosing change, these areas are triggered and will issue adrenalin-like hormones. Clients often re-live emotions which they first felt as children and may have hidden away in their Top Secret File or even in their locked trunk. Their attachment behaviour provides a clue to some of the hidden material and defence mechanisms may indicate suppressed feelings. As a coach, you will be aware of the anxiety in a client about the prospect of change if it triggers such a response. While not addressing the originating event (as a therapist), as coach you will work with the current event. The chapter is completed with a tour of defence mechanisms and the drama triangle.

4 Once more with feeling

In this chapter we discuss how you and your client manage emotions and then we discuss how to respond empathically to your client's feelings. Why are your own feelings relevant? First, this is where your emotional vocabulary originates, second, when you are unaware of your own feelings, they might be doing all sorts of things to other people without you realizing it.

When you are able to recognize your own feelings, it is easier to recognize others' feelings. Also if you have strong feelings which are unexpressed verbally, they have a nasty habit of leaking out non-verbally, so that they are visible to others. Being real in a coaching situation is one of Carl Rogers' conditions for effecting client change. So managing your own emotions will impact on your ability to be an effective coach.

The chapter describes the basics of empathy, including how to identify your client's feelings and the channels through which emotion is expressed. We give examples of the various degrees and modes of empathy, as well as a list of emotional vocabulary.

Managing emotion: self and others

Humans are emotional beings and express emotions easily from an early age and only control their expression as a consequence of growing up. Some of this control is necessary and proper for responsible adult life.

However, how a person is brought up does influence the development of emotional awareness. For example, if, as a child, you were punished for being sad, tearful, angry or even excited about certain things, you will have learned to control your expression of these feelings. Over time, you lose sight of the forbidden feelings and cannot bring them to mind. The punishment may not be traditional or corporal but withdrawal by a loved parent, signs of disapproval, or silent reproach are powerful messages to a growing person.

This life experience affects your self-image by suppressing unacceptable feelings – suppressing is a kind of forgetting. As youngsters, often without realizing it, you received messages about what was and was not acceptable. You can identify some of the messages in Figures 4.1 a), b), c) and d):

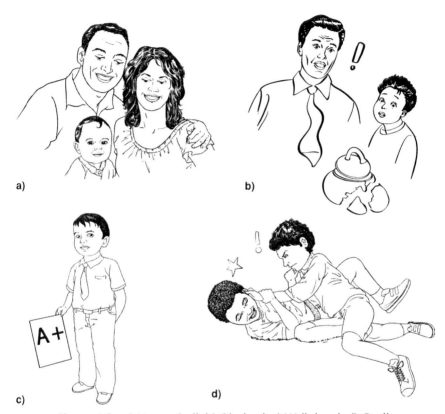

Figure 4.1   a) New arrival!, b) Oh dear!, c) Well done!, d) Grrr!!

The impact of these messages can persist into adulthood. As you grow up, you receive more messages from important others like parents and teachers which affect your self-image, and therefore your self-esteem. For example, you might grow up to believe yourself to be shy, dreamy, serious, impractical, clever, slow to learn, etc. Equally you may find it difficult to express justifiable frustration, anger or appropriate sadness.

Some people believe that human beings are born with a personality and it is true that there are identifiable aspects of personality which are genetic. This is nature. However, there is plenty of evidence that nurture plays a big part in how we finally mature. The nature/nurture argument continues and the reality is that if we were all fixed at birth, there would be no point in training or developmental coaching.

As youngsters, we absorb some of the messages of worth from parents or teachers and accept them as true. These will be positive as well as negative, e.g. we may believe we are artistic, intelligent, practical, limited, stupid, naughty, etc. Powerful messages can frighten a child and these may include 'don't cry, don't appear frightened or weak'. Some feelings are unacceptable and these will form our Top Secret File (Figure 4.2). Some feelings are so painful they are denied. Examples may include feelings of helplessness, being angry, crying, being sexual, etc. and these messages are stored in our locked trunk. The lock may be so strong that the feelings are beyond our awareness. When these denied feelings are triggered, we can experience distress and we may seek help through therapy.

Figure 4.2 The Top Secret File and the locked trunk

Later in life the contents may be questioned and revised so that a healthy self-image is formed. A healthy self-image grows from our positive life experiences: teachers, friends, lovers, work colleagues, coaches, mentors, etc.

Claire

Claire is a manager in the local leisure centre run by a national charitable trust. As the eldest in the family, Claire was expected to help with her younger siblings, when her father left. Claire's mother had always been unwell and Claire almost ran the household around attending school. If Claire ever seemed tired or impatient, her mother became ill and tearful so Claire's feelings of helplessness and her own neediness were hidden in her Top Secret File. When Claire begins to find that her mother's illness and home commitments are interfering with her job, she is unable to ask for help. She is determined to be the strong resourceful person which she has learnt is acceptable, and is unaware of her strong feelings about neediness. Claire is also unaware of her deep feelings of anger which come from her father's departure following a violent quarrel, after which her mother became permanently unwell. This is hidden away from her awareness in her locked trunk and might emerge in therapy.

If Claire becomes a coaching client, she may choose to work on being able to express her helpless feelings and find a way to meet her needs and perform at work. She may decide to confront her family and tell them what she wants in her life. Coaching with empathy can address her Top Secret File and enhance her self-image by acknowledging her right to ask for help.

Claire's upbringing included experience of violence and anger. Her fear of this makes her avoid and disapprove of anger. Her locked trunk may include this fear but is not accessible to her, as she says to people: 'I prefer not to be angry – it never solves anything.' Unfortunately the denied feelings are often 'leaked' in other ways, e.g. displaced or projected on to others and this can lead to difficulties at work or in relationships. The locked trunk material is suitable for therapy rather than coaching.

You may like to consider what might be in your Top Secret File as this is likely to affect your coaching. For example, a hidden fear of anger may prevent you recognizing it in their client or a hidden fear of weakness may mean that a tearful client is told to get over it.

> When James (our senior buyer in Chapter 2) begins to practise coaching with his team, his own feelings may affect his coaching. For example, when Helena bursts into tears, James is horrified and is unable to hide his reaction. When his young team members are giggling about his tailoring, he is aware of feeling rather hurt and when one of them persists in being jokey and sniggering in a coaching session, he feels quite annoyed. These reactions are part of James' own Top Secret File which hasn't prepared him for dealing with a weeping female, and includes a tendency to feel left out of things and impatient with people having fun.
>
> James discusses his feelings with his coach supervisor. They explore how he can handle tears and James learns to just listen when someone is upset, then offering empathy as 'You're upset because . . .'.
>
> Working in supervision James learns to 'park' his hurt feelings as these are not appropriate to share with a coachee. However, if James is able to be real and share his annoyance with his coachee, without scolding, he is actually giving his coachee feedback about the effect of his behaviour. He says: 'Look, Miles, I'm annoyed because this session is for your benefit and you don't seem to be valuing it.' When he does this, his junior buyers develop a bit more respect for him.

There is lots of evidence that self-image is influenced by gender, as the messages of worth we receive are different for males and females. In most cultures, boys and girls are brought up to express emotion differently. The Western norm for men as rational and unemotional, and women as emotional and non-rational, is the basis of many workplace difficulties for both genders. This has been described by Philip Hodson in his investigation into the emotional male (Hodson 1984) as a 'lethal role' for men as their health is affected by suppression or denial of their natural emotions. The emergence in the twenty-first century of a new man and a powerful woman is altering these preconceptions, but the changes are expressed more in social networking sites than the boardroom. Certain emotions are expressed differently in different cultures and as a coach you will need to be aware of this in cross-cultural work.

Decision-making is affected by emotions. Emotions are more powerful than rational analysis in decision-making. When the thinking mind dominates, and your client is 'choking on thought', they are less likely to be making effective decisions. Jonah Lehrer, a neuroscientist and humanities scholar, in his ground-breaking book, *The Decisive Moment,* showed that without our emotions we just cannot make up our mind (Lehrer 2009). What happens is a brain argument with the pre-frontal cortex struggling to resist the impulses coming from the limbic system and make a decision. The outcome is likely to be based on emotional reasons which the rational self may be unable to articulate. For instance, imaging has shown that consumers do not always purchase for rational reasons and political allegiances persist even when negative facts are known. In a series of brain-imaging experiments, when the limbic system is damaged, the person concerned is incapable of making a decision even though their rational cortex is present. For coaches this is explained well in Tim Gallwey's books, *The Inner Game of Tennis* (1974) and *The Inner Game of Work* (2000).

Because of the way your self-image is formed, some of your feelings may be suppressed or displaced. Hence as a coach you need to be alert to the possibility of emotions 'leaking' rather than being expressed directly by yourself in a coaching session. For example, you may inadvertently communicate impatience with your client by the pitch, tone or speed of your voice. The vocal channel is a favourite for leakage as we can convince ourselves that we didn't say anything negative – it's all in the voice.

In summary, feelings and emotions as basic human characteristics are neither good nor bad, right or wrong. As a learned style of behaviour, we show some of our emotions and not others, e.g. hurt, or anger often depending gender socialization. As a consequence we may not be able to handle it in others, and this has implications for you as coach when your client expresses their feelings. For instance, if your client becomes tearful, you might feel embarrassed and deal with the situation, by pretending it isn't happening or being overly sympathetic. As a skilled coach, you will allow the expression to occur without intervening. A good coach supervisor is a useful sounding board for which feelings are appropriate to express to a client. Where your coaching work triggers deep feelings which trouble you and may be based on material in your locked trunk, your supervisor may recommend that you seek therapy.

Communicating your emotions

When you think about speeches which have touched you and influenced you, what do you remember? For many people, the address of Martin Luther King from the balcony of the Lincoln Memorial is memorable because he spoke from the heart about his feelings and his dream. American President John F. Kennedy's 'Ich bin ein Berliner' speech during the Cold War had a huge impact because it spoke of feelings.

Almost certainly the presenter who has the most impact will express emotion effectively *and appropriately* as part of their presentation. They may admit to feeling daunted by their task; they may disclose a relevant emotional part of their lives; they may express their passion and enthusiasm for their subject. So presenters who can communicate a range of emotions are effective speakers, indeed, those who train presenters in public speaking use this in their training programmes.

What is an appropriate expression of emotion? When we express emotion, we disclose a part of ourselves which is important to us, so sometimes we over-do it and it may be inappropriate to do so at that time or in that place or in that way. Appropriate means that the emotion is expressed at the right depth, length, target, time and place. We have all experienced a fellow passenger who describes at length their recent operation in full medical details to complete strangers in a crowded commuter train. On the other hand, your best friend may choose to confide a critical issue with you in a quiet coffee bar where you have met after work.

The emotional channels

We express emotion through three channels: verbal, non-verbal and vocal. Where certain emotions are not acceptable, they will not be mentioned in words, but they will 'leak' through the non-verbal channel and, where this has become controlled, ultimately, the vocal channel. For many women, expressing anger is difficult as social norms dictate an ideal woman should not be angry. The ideal allows her to be tearful and this may indicate anger being expressed. The ideal male in the Western world is rational and unemotional, so for many men crying in public is not allowed, except in very specific circumstances.

You may wish to identify when is it OK in your culture for men to cry in public? When is it OK for women to be openly angry in public? Why is this important?

If you wish to access the emotional world of your client, you will need to be aware of potential leaking, as their suppressed emotions are likely to be the ones which are influencing your client. This is often expressed by your client in terms such as: 'I don't know what came over me'; 'I can't understand it'; 'I surprised myself', etc. You may also want to be aware of when you yourself are leaking emotion in a coaching session.

We now examine the three channels.

The verbal channel: emotional language

Depending on your upbringing and education, you will have acquired an emotional vocabulary and you can identify how balanced yours is by listing all the feeling words you can think of under 'positive' and 'negative'.

Most people in the Western world have many more negative feeling words than positive ones. You can further divide your emotional vocabulary using the exercise in the box.

My emotional vocabulary

Make headings 'MAD BAD SAD GLAD' across the top of your page. Then just freely associate with those headings, writing underneath the feeling words which come to mind instantly. Keep going for as long as you can, being careful not to include thinking or doing words, only feeling words for this exercise. When you run out of ideas, compare your lists and see which column is the longest and which the shortest. Then you have a sense of the balance in your emotional vocabulary. Table 4.1 on p. 86 is an example of what it should look like.

We provide a sample list of feeling words and some metaphors, in Table 4.1 on p. 86. When feelings are suppressed, people resort to expressing themselves through non-feelings and one of these is metaphor. We discuss non-feelings below in the section entitled 'The basics of empathy'.

The verbal channel may carry emotions through local sayings which have special meanings. For example, your client may say: 'I was dossing' which may mean 'I was avoiding work' rather than staying in a doss-house; or 'we will bake the brand' and 'footprint' which are used to mean something other than cooking or walking ('bake' is internet language for development of a brand idea; 'footprint' means the space for reception of an electronic signal). Here the well-known method of re-statement ensures that you and your client have a shared understanding of the issue. Details for re-statement as a skill can be found in Brockbank and McGill (2012).

Why is the verbal channel important? When your client is expressing their emotions non-verbally or vocally, in order to offer them empathy, you will need to find words to describe the feeling as well as what you see or hear. This is primary empathy where you respond to emotions expressed *in some way* by your client and this was explained on p. 6. When you wish to be real with your client, your expression of emotion needs to be at the correct level, so that you don't say 'I'm feeling angry' when you are just feeling irritated or impatient. For coaches who never feel impatient or irritated, this book is not necessary.

Your client may use metaphors to express their emotions, saying perhaps, 'It was like a cold shower' and you can use these words in your empathy or connect them to what has already been said, e.g. 'You felt disheartened.'

The non-verbal channel

The non-verbal channel is everything else which is not words. The channel is the face and body. Emotion is expressed in facial expressions like smiling, grimacing or frowning and by eye contact, or lack of it, as shown in Figure 4.3.

a) smile with no eye contact

b) smile with eye contact

c) frown and no smile with eye contact

d) frown and no smile with no eye contact

Figure 4.3 The non-verbal channel: facial expressions

The connections between facial expressions and feelings are similar in different cultures. Leaked emotions may be spotted in the face, and researchers have proved that even when the expression occurs in a micro-second, the viewer 'spots' it and may respond to it, without even being aware of having seen it. Clients may try to hide an unacceptable emotion by covering their face, eyes or mouth with their hands. Upbringing may lead to the masking of certain emotions, so that people can be seen smiling while describing a sad event. As a coach you are unlikely to be able to hide strong emotion so we recommend being real if at all possible.

Bodily gestures that carry emotion include posture and movement such as a position which appears closed or open. Limb movement may suggest feelings, like hands, legs or feet fidgeting as in Figure 4.4.

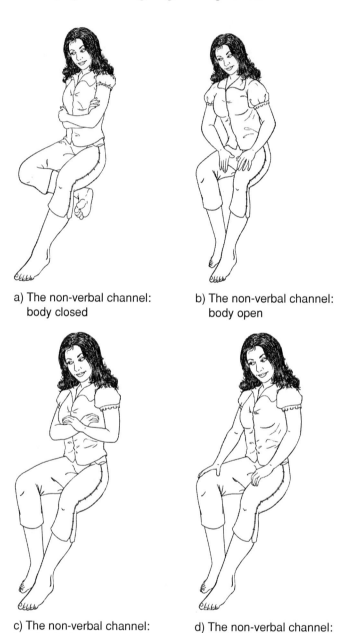

a) The non-verbal channel:
   body closed

b) The non-verbal channel:
   body open

c) The non-verbal channel:
hand wringing

d) The non-verbal channel:
   foot or leg tapping

Figure 4.4   The non-verbal channel

Where clients have learned to suppress or deny unacceptable emotions, and these emotions are pressing for expression, they can appear in different ways, such as wringing hands, tapping feet, bouncing legs, folded arms, head drooping, and the like. Some body positions are culture-specific, like the distance between people and relative positioning. For example, bowing is a greeting in some cultures and not others. Standing too near someone is considered rude in almost all cultural contexts, and can only be tolerated if other cues like eye contact are removed, as in a crowded train or elevator.

The vocal channel

This is the overlooked channel, but often carries strong emotion, especially where your client is suppressing open expression of emotion. The vocal channel is where your client cannot lie and the tone, pitch, volume, pace and style of this channel may communicate their feelings to you.

For instance, when someone is being sarcastic, all the message is carried by the vocal channel, as the verbal channel denies what is being communicated, e.g. 'That went well' or 'That's a nice way to behave!' Examples of vocal expression of emotion include differences in volume, pitch, speed and what is known as 'paralanguage'. This is use of slang, hesitation, stuttering, repetition and what are known as Freudian slips. For example, if your client says 'She is so lucky I could kill her' you may like to guess at the feeling hidden in the slip. So your client may shout or whisper, clients may squeak with fear or surprise; a scolding or passive tone; clients who rush their story, etc.

Awareness of your own emotional state

Awareness of your own emotional state is a key ability for coaches. When you are able to express clearly in words what it is you are feeling and why, you will be confident with others' expressions of emotion. You may have difficulty expressing some emotions or express them indirectly, e.g. you may feel frustrated or impatient, and if not expressed, this may be leaked in your voice or body language. You may be daunted by the seniority or power of your client and expressing this is preferable to leaking it. On the other hand, you may judge that the feeling should be 'parked' and we discuss this below.

We refer now to the difficult/easy continuum shown in Figure 4.5, based on a diagram by Gerard Egan, a professor of organizational development and well known for his work on relationship skills. Figure 4.5 indicates how awkward we find emotional expression, by ourselves and by or to others. For example, expressing or receiving a positive emotion from a person who is present is the most difficult. This is why some managers are unable to deliver praise directly. The easiest situation is negative emotion about a person who is absent – this is gossip. An understanding of this continuum will enable you as coach to anticipate what is happening to your client. Note: when an emotion is described as positive or negative this refers to how we judge it – the emotion itself is neither right nor wrong.

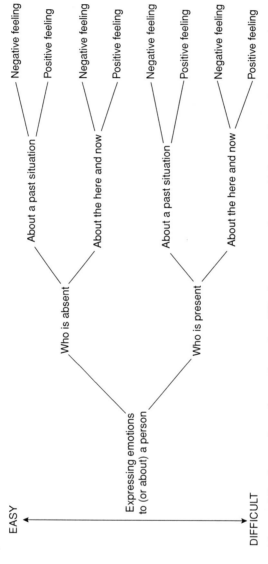

Figure 4.5 Expression of emotion: the difficult–easy continuum (Adapted from Egan 1977:81, in Brockbank and McGill 1998)

The diagram suggests that (in the Western world) we find it easier to express negative emotion and this is borne out by our lop-sided emotional vocabulary which tends to incorporate more negative feelings than positive ones, so as a coach you will need to develop a positive emotional vocabulary. Also the diagram shows that by being able to express emotions about people in their absence more easily than to their face, you may avoid expressing feelings in the here and now, and this is true for your client as well.

Why should we express feelings – can't they just be ignored?

Storing or parking

Storing up emotions is not helpful generally, for when they eventually erupt, they may explode and this is nicely stated by William Blake:

I was angry with my friend;
I told my wrath, my wrath did end;
I was angry with my foe;
I told it not, my wrath did grow.

(The Poison Tree by William Blake 1756–1827)

In our day-to-day life we make a judgement about whether our expression of emotion is appropriate as above:

- To whom am I expressing the feeling?
- What length is enough?
- How deep can I go with this person?
- Is this the right time?

We can unconsciously judge whether the person concerned can cope with hearing about our feelings. For example, you may decide that a formal meeting is not the best place to take up your frustration with your colleague and park it for a later more suitable time. When you meet her later, you see that she seems agitated – you decide to keep your expression of annoyance as low key as possible, explaining simply how you are affected by her behaviour.

Although it is usually better to express feelings as they arise even if they seem negative, as a skilled coach, you may decide to park them, raise them later, or take them to your coach supervisor. On the other hand, if your client struggles to express emotion appropriately, you are able to provide a model for them. For example, you may say: 'I am feeling confused – have I missed something here?' to give your client an example of low-key emotion expressed without risk, by taking responsibility for the feeling.

Other people's emotions

Emotional expressions in others can be disturbing, often triggering a negative response, learned early in life. This accounts for the disapproval of 'pushy' or angry women, and of weak or tearful men. Managers presented with staff in tears find this difficult. Passive male team members are discounted, while assertive behaviour in women can seem aggressive. Many of these reactions are part of a cultural heritage which is common to our family, colleagues and friends.

How you respond to a particular emotion in yourself affects how you react to the same emotion expressed by others. The good news is that this has been learned, so if not serving you well, can be unlearned. A responsible coach should be aware of what is in their own Top Secret File (and ideally some of what is in their locked trunk), bearing in mind that not many of us manage to have a totally healthy self-image. Regular supervision will ensure that as a coach you are aware of the contents of your Top Secret File and, if necessary, your locked file.

Effective empathy, an understanding of your own emotional world, will enable you to 'park' your instinctive responses and attend to your client. This does not mean your own feelings are dismissed – they are simply parked temporarily. One way to describe this is to be double-minded, i.e. attend to the other as well as yourself rather than being single-minded. When your attention is single-minded, you are attending only to yourself and your empathy is switched off.

Difficult questions to be answered in this situation are: What emotion do you think should be parked by a coach? Whatever the emotional expression by your client, how can you respond with empathy?

The basics of empathy

As mentioned in Chapter 1, many people are puzzled about what empathy is, confusing it with sympathy or pity. Our experience of training also suggests that deliberate empathy may feel strange at first and coaches tend to feel embarrassed by doing it.

Definition of empathy

On p. 2 we defined empathy as:

> An understanding of the world from the other's point of view, their feelings, experience and behaviour, and *the communication of that understanding to the other in full.*

Thus, as a coach, empathy is:

- what your client is feeling or felt or may feel (expressed by your client in words or non-verbal behaviour);
- the experience and/or behaviour which is the source of that feeling (revealed by what your client has already said);
- communication of that information in full.

To give an empathic response to your client, you need to identify your client's feeling, the source of that feeling and then communicate both in speech. Empathy to be effective and skilful needs to be operational, i.e. it must be expressed and it must be received by your client to be any use.

Identifying feelings

Feelings are expressed differently by each client, in terms of their gender, age, race, social class, education, status and cultural background, as well as their stage of development as a person (not necessarily the same as maturity).

Gender is a typical example of how feelings are expressed differently. The male role in Western society has been described as 'lethal' because of its characteristic suppression of emotion and its negative impact on health and well-being. Age and maturity tend to magnify gender effects so that older men and some women, traditionally reared, will tend to carry on with their unemotional behaviour, except for those who are lucky enough to experience relational therapy or effective coaching and access their emotional world. Modern career women, in order to succeed in male-dominated professions, may suppress emotion at work, while many women choose caring professions as they are more comfortable where emotional expression is the norm. Racial awareness training frequently identifies perceptions of black people as more emotionally expressive than their white counterparts, and this is often viewed negatively. Your client's social class or status in society may also influence their degree of emotional expressiveness.

Surprisingly, education is negatively correlated with expression of emotion. The education offered in Western Europe takes children who are born as free expressers of emotion and develops them into fully locked-in mature adults! The (Western) world of academia has focused on thinking almost exclusively since the eleventh century, exemplified by the great thinkers, Thomas Aquinas and René Descartes.

Dr James Hemming (1909–2007) was President and later Vice-President of the British Humanist Association. He was a dedicated teacher and psychologist and a passionate advocate of an education system that would value and encourage every child. His book, *The Betrayal of Youth* (1980) argues passionately for an education which includes emotion. Many of his ideas on education remain all too relevant today. He criticized an education system designed mainly to produce measurable results and proposed a curriculum which would mobilize all pupils' resources, social and emotional as much as mental, and encourage them to see themselves as competent. The psycho-therapist, Susie Orbach has urged policy-makers in every field to prioritize emotional literacy in order to address the levels of distress in people's working lives.

At one extreme are those whose early life experience includes separation from home and parental love (boarding school) and, at the other, are those whose early life experience was limited by extreme poverty or even abuse.

David

David was sent to boarding school in England while his parents lived and worked abroad. There was plenty of money but David was bullied unmercifully and it got worse if he cried or pleaded, so he learnt to hide his distress. When his parents visited him, they discouraged any soppiness and his father would say: 'Chin up, old man' as they left him again, and he learnt to hide his longing for a cuddle.

Ron

Ron was the elder of two and the only boy. His father was aggressive and beat him as a child 'for his own good'. He would hide in a cupboard to avoid his violence. Ron developed a tough persona and a thuggish exterior which hid his true hurt and deep lonely feelings. As an adult, he was pushy, insulting and aggressive, particularly to women colleagues.

Such clients may look surprised by an enquiry about their feelings as they are pretty sure they don't have any, so you must be careful with questioning. Through coaching work using empathy the clients may discover some of their feelings. For David, his intolerance of his own feelings of abandonment makes him impatient with staff who appear distressed. For Ron, his own hurt is well hidden by his macho exterior, and he has no time for any wimpish behaviour by his staff. Coaching can address David's Top Secret File. However, the eruption of feelings for such a client may well be so intense that there is need for therapy. Guidance for referral can be found in Chapter 8.

Finally, the cultural background of your client may influence the degree to which they feel free to express emotion. For instance, some cultures discourage the expression of anger, others discourage displays of distress or enthusiasm, and coaches need to be aware of the cultural norms in their client's life.

The verbal channel is where your client is likely to either express emotion in words or avoid expressing emotion in words. What does this mean? Your client may begin with 'I feel' but move onto an opinion, a thought, a judgement, a criticism or an evaluation, rather than expressing their true feelings. For instance, 'I feel' may be followed by the words 'like', 'as if', 'you', 'he', 'she', 'they', 'that', 'it', and none of these will be followed by feelings. They will be followed by a thought or opinion. Follow these examples carefully and you will see how they are not true expressions of feelings.

- I feel like I am always in the wrong (a judgement).
- I feel it is unfair to change the rota (an opinion).
- I feel she was rather domineering in the meeting (criticism or compliment?).
- I feel he didn't stand up for himself in the meeting (criticism or compliment?).
- I feel you ignored me (a judgement).
- I feel it is ineffective (an evaluation).
- I feel they are not pulling their weight (an opinion).
- I feel as if I am just not important in this team (a thought).

And the one most familiar in today's world …

- I feel that …

As soon as you hear the word 'that', you know you will hear a thought/belief/opinion, not a feeling.

You may like to guess at the real feelings behind these statements and use them in the practice run below.

Another way of expressing emotion is the PP expression of feeling. PP stands for Past Participle (the past form of a verb) and will be familiar to coaches using goal-setting techniques. You will always ask your client to state their goal in terms of a Past participle (in bold in the bullet list of examples) like:

- Report **completed** by …
- My weight **reduced** by …
- Customer ratings **increased** by …

The clue to a PP is that it ends in 'ed'.

How does someone use the Past Participle to express a feeling? They might say:

I feel intimidated.

This suggests that there is someone out there who is intimidating them and as coach you will need to use advanced empathy in this situation and you need to be very careful. We give a tip about this below.

As mentioned above, the most used method of avoiding direct expression of emotion is the use of 'I feel that ...' How is this different from 'I feel ...'?

> I feel ... (a word which describes their feeling)
> I feel that ... is always followed by a thought, opinion or belief.

With the first, your client is in touch with their feelings and you will be able to use their words in your empathic response (see pages 7 and 8). However, your client's emotional vocabulary may be limited and they say: 'I feel that ...', an increasingly popular expression in modern conversation. 'I feel that' phrases can never express a feeling, only a thought or opinion. The real feeling is given in brackets in the examples below.

- I feel that the room is overheated (I feel too hot – an easy one).
- I feel that you let me down (I feel disappointed – maybe could be angry or sad).
- I feel that a decision is urgent now (I feel anxious or impatient?).
- I feel that he should have said something (I feel annoyed, disappointed?).
- I feel that the staff took this too seriously (I feel ... surprised?).
- I feel that the event went well enough (I feel pleased, satisfied?).

The difficulty with 'I feel that ...' is that it cannot express a feeling. Test this for yourself. Place a word which describes a feeling after 'I feel that ...' and see if the statement makes any sense:

- I feel that – annoyed.
- I feel that – worried.
- I feel that – angry.
- I feel that – happy.
- I feel that – unsure.
- I feel that – excited.

So frequently your client will give you the 'I feel that ...' version so that the feeling is not clear. Why do people say 'I feel' and then don't declare their feeling?

The reason is a good one – they want their statement to be accepted and the best way to do that is to express it as a feeling because it is not possible to disagree with a feeling. With a clear statement of opinion, a belief or a thought, there is room for disagreement, even argument, but with feelings they are just there and are personal to the speaker. Another reason for 'I feel that …' is to soften what may actually be a judgemental or prejudiced state-ment, e.g. 'I feel that foreigners are taking all our jobs' may be easier to say than 'I feel angry about or threatened by immigrants'.

When your client uses 'I feel that …' and avoids expressing their feeling directly, they are likely to be expressing it either non-verbally or vocally, i.e. their face, body or voice will carry the emotion. Here the coach needs to be careful – in the example above we have guessed at the client's feelings of anger or threat about immigrants based on the words they used. Only the coach in the room will see the leaked emotion in their client. For example, you may see that your client becomes heated, with a red face, shouting voice, punching the air, quicker speech or stumbling over some words, and these are expres-sions of anger or fear.

The non-verbal channel will display emotions through facial expressions as above, body movements and posture or positioning of limbs, head or trunk. The vocal channel will express emotion as shouting, whispering, speaking very quickly or slowly, etc.

Having identified your client's feelings and the reasons for them you are ready to respond with empathy.

Levels of empathy

There are different levels of empathy, ranging from 0 to 3, and it is up to the coach to judge which level to use according to the context.

> 0 Zero: questions, judgements, advice, etc. see the list below.
> 1 Partial: one identified feeling out of two or more.
> 2 Primary: based on verbal or non-verbal expression of emotion or feeling.
> 3 Advanced: a guess or 'felt' sense of a feeling or feelings.

Zero empathy

Zero empathy is just what it says – no empathy. Instead of empathy, a coach may offer many other responses and there may be good reasons for this option. Some alternatives are listed in the example below.

> Your client says, while spreading out both hands, 'Look I am fed up with the stock being misplaced. We need a better system. I end up being blamed. That manager is out to get me.'

This statement can be followed by a number of other responses, including:

- the cliché;
- questioning;
- interpretation;

- inaccurate statements;
- different language;
- giving advice;
- giving an evaluation;
- making a judgement;
- challenging.

You may respond with a *cliché* like, 'I hear what you say' or 'I understand' which in themselves are of no help to your client. Such statements do not convey to your client that they are understood. They are more likely to convey that they are *not* understood as you have not included the strong emotional content of your client's statement in your response.

A *questioning* response to your client's statement might be, 'In what ways are you blamed?' The question (which may be relevant) does not convey empathic support about how and whether you are understanding their position.

Interpreting your client's words occurs when you respond by trying to guess what is implied in the disclosure. An example might be, 'What do you mean by blamed?'

Your response may just be plainly *inaccurate* like, 'You're not very happy with the way your work is going.'

You may use language that is *very different* to your client. Using similar language in response to that used by your client encourages rapport provided the language you use is authentic to you. You can then convey that you are in tune with your client. See Chapter 5 for more on this.

You can reply by *giving advice*, e.g. 'Oh dear, you mustn't worry – you will be fine if you follow the merchandising diagram.'

Judging what the speaker has said, e.g. 'Blaming sounds rather inflammatory.'

Or

Challenging the speaker, e.g. 'I bet you can't prove that.'

Partial empathy

Partial empathy is a form of primary empathy so you are responding to an expressed feeling by your client. However, there may be other feelings expressed which you may miss or choose to leave aside.

> Your client may be saying, while spreading out both hands, 'Look I am fed up with the stock being misplaced. We need a better system. I end up being blamed. That manager is out to get me.'

A partial empathy response might be: 'You're fed up with stock being misplaced and you'd like a better system', which recognizes their feeling of being fed up, the reason for it, and the communication of both to your client. This fulfils the three components of empathy, but is partial because it does not include the emotion expressed in the outspread hands or their feelings about their manager. So partial empathy is good, but not enough for developmental work. However, it is totally appropriate for performance work.

Primary empathy

Primary empathy includes communication of all the feelings expressed by your client, the reasons for these feelings, and a response which identifies them accurately. For example, a response to the client above could be: 'You're fed up and impatient with the current stock system and you'd like a better one.'

But what if your client denies their feeling?

The important factor in primary empathy is evidence. You should be able to support your response by describing what you see and hear. In this case you noticed that your client has spread their hands, showing their impatience. Your client may still deny their feeling, especially if it is unacceptable to them. Often your client will come back to that feeling as your understanding promotes trust and safety.

Advanced empathy

Advanced empathy is a response for which there may not be sufficient evidence about a possible feeling in your client and you can be mistaken. This is sometimes described as a 'felt sense'. For example, a further response to the client above, to include their comment about their manager, could be: 'You feel blamed because you are responsible for the section. You seem rather wary of your manager.'

When a client uses the PP (past participle) expression of emotion, a top tip for empathy is to use 'because' like this:

You feel blamed … because …

The unfinished sentence leaves a space for your client to fill if they choose to do so. Other examples of PP responses are:

You feel intimidated … because …
You feel excited … because …

You may of course provide the reason if you have guessed it.

Advanced empathy relies on really good listening skills which include observing the body and face of your client, their voice and their demeanour. In addition, you will have heard from your client many things which add to your guess. Fundamentally truly attending to your client will enable you to offer advanced empathy.

Your client may not agree with your guess. This doesn't matter, as nine times out of ten, they will then tell you what their true feeling is. For example, the employee above may say 'No, I'm not wary – I'm furious.'

The important factor in advanced empathy is lack of evidence and therefore the response must be *tentative*. Use of qualifiers like 'I guess', 'perhaps', 'I wonder', 'you seem' and 'could it be' will make your response tentative. This enables your client to agree or disagree and maybe clarify, expressing the real feeling they have and then your response can be primary empathy.

Modes of empathy

Clients express emotions which they have felt in the past, or in the present or are likely to feel in the future. So empathy may be offered in three modes:

Past
Present
Future

Past mode

You felt ... when ... because ...
You were feeling ... because ...

Present mode

You feel ... because ...
You're feeling ... because ...
You feel ... when ... because ...

Future mode

You may feel ... because ...
You may feel ... when ... because ...
You are likely to feel ... when ... because ...
You're expecting to feel ...

The three modes of empathy are needed to use the NEWW model explained in Chapter 6. The coach recognizes their clients' feelings in the here and now.

The N is for Now of the model. In the case above, the coach said, 'You feel fed up' in the here and now. Empathy in past mode is used when the client talks about their past and this is the E for Empathy in the model. In the case above, the coach said, 'You felt blamed.' Feelings in any future actions will emerge as the coaching proceeds to how she will deal with her manager and may include:

> It sounds like you may feel scared to confront him.
> You seem to be expecting to feel angry when you meet him.
> Given our discussion, you are likely to feel determined when it happens.

Coaches may tend to favour responding to positive feelings and ignore negative ones, believing that this helps clients towards productive action. This may not help in particular coaching situations, for example:

> Ann is coaching students in a Belgian college, who are re-sitting their business exams, having been downgraded and not allowed to proceed. Her students are ethnically diverse so she is careful to attend to cultural differences, which may include excessive fear of failure. She establishes relationships by accepting their disappointment, before attending to their difficulties and sharing some of her own experience. She works with their struggles rather than jollying them along and this involves responding to their fears as well as their confidence as young business women.
>
> (Ann de Kock, college lecturer)

> Rose coaches youngsters with physical and mental special needs at a local gymnastics club. Members regularly achieve national and international championship level. Sometimes, after a period of good performance, her clients can lose heart, feeling limited by their disability. Rose works with their feelings, reading their face and voice, listening to 'I can't do that' and insisting on connecting with them. She is keen to establish boundaries and understands when her clients are afraid of looking foolish or are getting over-excited. She earns their trust by her consistent empathy and supporting them physically where appropriate. She tells her clients that she will push them to achieve success and will never give up on them.
>
> (Rose Ricks, club coach)

Where coaches are working with resistance or even disability, they should not be afraid to recognize negative feelings. Clients often struggle to find a word to describe their feeling, and the coach may need to supply a word when the client is avoiding expression of it. To help with this a list of feeling words is given in Table 4.1.

Table 4.1 Feelings vocabulary (arranged top down from low to high intensity)

MAD	SAD	GLAD	EXCITED	CONCERNED	BAD
irritated	upset	happy	positive	fed up	disgusted
annoyed	hopeless	satisfied	interested	anxious	scared
tetchy	useless	pleased	energetic	worried	negative
grumpy	disappointed	content	engaged	uncomfortable	intimidated
bad-tempered	depressed	comfortable	enthusiastic	dissatisfied	afraid
frustrated	lonely	delighted	entranced	disturbed	horrified
angry	tearful	hopeful	intoxicated	pressured	sick
irate	hurt	valued	fizzy	stressed	revolted
furious	betrayed	joyful	curious	alarmed	resentful
livid	pained	useful	fascinated	troubled	bitter
enraged	miserable	thrilled	stimulated	distracted	trapped
furious	desperate	ecstatic			
Metaphors					
Fit to kill	at rock bottom	cat with two tails	on cloud nine	in two minds	like nothing
Ready to burst	let down	happy as a lark	over the moon	sick as a parrot	

Summary

In this chapter we have stressed the need for a coach to be aware of their own feelings and how they are expressing them. Feelings are expressed through three channels, not just in words. The chapter gives examples of zero, partial, primary and advanced empathy as well as a list of feeling words. Zero empathy is the absence of empathy and a coach may offer many other responses. Partial empathy responds to only part of what has been expressed and this may be a sensible response in particular situations. Primary empathy responds to feelings and experience which have been expressed explicitly, while advanced empathy endeavours to 'read between the lines' or respond to feelings which may have been expressed obliquely. However, because we inhabit an environment which largely devalues feeling and emotion, some advanced empathy skills may be needed where your client is suppressing or denying what they are clearly feeling. This is particularly important when you are dealing with conflict, calling for the ability to challenge. We discuss how to do this in Chapter 7.

5 Questioning: why are you asking?

In this chapter we discuss the reasons for questions and what makes you want to question your client. We recommend that questions take second place to empathy so that they can benefit rather than hamper the coaching relationship. We also suggest that empathy + questioning is a more rapid method to facilitate change. We examine the purpose and impact of a range of questions and techniques including surface/deep structures, Clean Language and the Byron Katie questions.

Questioning is an important element in many situations, like witness reporting, police investigations, government surveys, legal action and medical histories. Perhaps because of this connection, questioning for some clients may seem intrusive or even threatening. For many people, questions in school were linked with knowing the right answer or not. So questions can feel like a test and people often say when they are questioned that they are in the hot seat. Some managers may question their staff into submission, and this is unlikely to lead to co-operation.

However, questioning is also the mainstay of your coaching sessions, as it enables you to collect information, invite reflection, challenge discrepancy, check progress, and re-state some of the tfgs in your client's situation.

As a coach, you must clarify the goals of the coaching and identify the context in which you are working. This needs to be checked out so that you know the type of coaching to use, and therefore the level of empathy which is appropriate. For example, as a line manager you will need to establish that your staff understand the objectives of their work. For performance management, you will need to question your staff about their key performance indicators before discussing their performance.

Peter

Peter manages a team of claim negotiators in an insurance company, Charlotte being one of them. In his weekly one-to-one session with Charlotte, he checks out her understanding of the weekly claim-to-settlement targets for her section. He will say: 'Let's just check we are on the same page, what is the weekly target for your accounts?'

Similarly for engagement coaching, you will want to establish what your client understands about company objectives.

> When Peter holds a management briefing with his team, he checks out their knowledge of the objectives for the team before moving towards how the team may contribute to them. He may begin by saying, 'Good morning, team, can anyone tell me where we are with the monthly claim-to-settlement targets?'

When you are commissioned as an executive coach, it is no use assuming that the sponsor's goals are also your client's. A three-way meeting with the sponsor and the client is a good way to clarify whose goals the coaching is for, although there is always room for these to change.

> For example, Martin, an executive coach, was commissioned by Kate, the HR manager in an insurance firm, to work with Peter who is an experienced loss adjuster, leading a team of claim negotiators. Peter has applied twice for promotion to manage the entire Commercial Risks Claims Section, but was unsuccessful while his younger colleague, Della got the job. Peter is now Della's direct report and because she is not happy with his performance, she has asked Kate in HR to buy in coaching support for him.
>
> His management style is giving rise to complaints from his very go-getting young team members. They are all keen to collect their commission on referrals but are often kept waiting for the next client case. Peter, who is rather laid-back, refuses to be hurried and they are frustrated. Martin asks Kate to arrange a three-way meeting between Martin himself, Peter (client) and Della (Peter's manager).
>
> Della insists on seeing Martin before the meeting and Martin wisely insists on this meeting, and any others, being included in his contract. Della gives Martin the history of her relationship with Peter and her issues with his work. Martin establishes that he will not try to manage Peter, and suggests that Della works with Peter on their relationship. She says she is too busy to waste time on touchy-feely coaching. Martin suggests that the coaching can aim to improve Peter's engagement with his work and the company. They agree on an outcome measure based on fewer complaints from Peter's team members. When the three-way meeting takes place, Della repeats her concerns and Peter, rather meekly agrees to the coaching objectives.

As this appears to be engagement coaching, Martin will use primary empathy particularly at the first session where the relationship with Peter will begin. As and when Peter generates his own objectives, the coaching will become developmental. What about questioning? Doesn't Martin need to check out Peter's attitude to the coaching?

You will need questioning to explore your client's situation, what is happening to your client and what affects their learning, be it improvement or development. In addition, your questioning is needed to ascertain the agreed actions which will follow from the coaching so that your client leaves with an action plan of some kind.

All too often, however, questioning does not come with empathy and then it may be experienced as potentially intrusive. When empathy precedes your question, the impact of your question is enhanced. When you offer empathic understanding first, a change takes place in your client and their receptivity to your question is heightened. We recommend that questions are always preceded by empathy at the right level for the coaching context.

> In this case, Martin finds that he has no need to question Peter as he enters the room noisily, slams the door and flings himself down in a chair. Martin says: 'You don't seem too happy with what we are doing here.'
>
> Peter says: 'Too right, I'm not! She got the job and now she wants to push me around.'
>
> Martin continues: 'You sound quite angry' and Peter agrees by saying, 'Why should I bother? They don't appreciate me here.' Martin waits and Peter says with clenched hands and teeth, 'I don't see why I should support her career when mine is trashed.'
>
> An empathic response could be 'I guess you resent having to support her career when she got the promotion over you.'

Questioning is often focused on the need to know, and, in a bid for more information and to identify potential action points, a necessary process. Empathy, however, focuses on the feelings, and opens the gateway to a client's ability to change something about themselves. Neuroscience has established that the emotional brain holds more power for decisions and change than the thinking brain. See Chapter 3 for a discussion of this. Hence the emotional domain is the most important for learning and development. This is not to dismiss the importance of the knowing and action domains. In empathic coaching, these follow quite naturally from the client's commitment to change, which is linked to their feelings rather than their thoughts or actions.

Types of question used in coaching

There are several types of question which can be used for coaching and we discuss them now. Questions can be classified as:

- open
- closed

- multiple
- rhetorical
- leading.

Aren't open questions empathic? No.

Socrates and the so-called open question

Socrates was a philosopher, who lived 2500 years ago in ancient Greece, a citizen of Athens, and he operated rather like a developmental coach. He had no school or company, no fees, he coached in the street and scorned professional teachers, claiming: 'I have no knowledge beyond my own ignorance.'

The 'naïve' question can be very powerful in development coaching in getting beyond 'the taken-for-granteds'.

His coaching influenced young people to achieve 'the need of knowing themselves' not unlike the purpose of developmental coaching today. He was so successful with this activity that he made enemies of some of his colleagues. When Athens went into a recession, they turned on Socrates and he was indicted on two charges:

- impiety – denying the official gods;
- corruption of youth – encouraging young men to criticize the existing order.

At the age of 70, Socrates was found guilty by the first democratic court in history and condemned to death. The execution was delayed, giving Socrates the opportunity to drink hemlock at sunset on a day and place of his choice. To read more about this fascinating 2500-year-old coach, a great book by Bettany Hughes entitled *The Hemlock Cup* may interest you.

Socratic questioning has the potential to take your client into a place where they begin to doubt previously held assumptions. The tfgs are being questioned and this is far from comfortable. In an imaginary dialogue with his friend Meno, Socrates demonstrated how to use open questions in his dialogue with a slave who knew nothing and had no education.

Socrates showed how the slave could understand geometry by open questioning alone. In the story the boy struggles with new ideas, and Socrates' friend Meno observes that the process is uncomfortable for the boy who is learning something completely new, compared to his previous comfortable state of ignorance: 'What advances he has made ... he did not know at first, and he does not know now ... but then he thought he knew ... and felt no difficulty ... now he feels a difficulty' (Hughes 2010: 282). This is a near-perfect description of what occurs in really effective developmental coaching. The discomfort is a sign that your client is doubting their previously believed tfgs.

Martin and Peter have established a good relationship. Martin allows Peter to express more of his feelings about not being promoted, saying: 'You feel overlooked and undervalued because Della was appointed instead of you.' When Martin moves towards the agreed objectives, he meets resistance from Peter who says, rather quickly and loudly, 'I want to do well for my team but I'm damned if I'll support her career' [meaning Della]. Martin says: 'You are angry about her being promoted over you – no wonder you feel resentful.' Peter says: 'You really do understand – I appreciate that.'

Martin continues: 'Where does this place you as lead loss adjuster for commercial claims?' and Peter replies: 'Not doing so well and unlikely to be promoted next time.' Martin says: 'What can you do about that?' Peter says: 'I need to get over it, don't I? But I can tell you, this isn't easy.'

An empathic response to this could be, 'You're ready to deal with how you feel but I sense you're not sure yet.'

Open questions

> I had six honest serving men
> They taught me all I knew.
> Their names were what and why and when and
> how and where and who.

(Rudyard Kipling)

This memorable rhyme gives six words to use in questioning and the idea of an open question. Such a question cannot be answered by a simple 'yes' or 'no'. So 'Do you understand what is needed?' can be answered by yes or no and is not an open question. It is a closed question. The use of Kipling's words enables you to avoid flagrantly closed questions. However, your open question may mask a hidden statement.

An apparently open question may have a statement behind it, e.g. when Della asks Peter, 'How can you improve the notification to settlement intervals in your portfolio?' The statement behind her question is likely to be 'Your settlement intervals are not good enough.'

Given their fragile relationship, Peter's response is likely to be: 'I don't know. You're the boss, you tell me.' If Della opens her meeting with Peter by saying: 'Tell me about the notification to settlement intervals last month.' Peter grudgingly responds with a figure and Della may be able to respond with empathy, saying: 'You must be disappointed' before asking 'What happened?'

Then and only then is the right time for the questions 'How can you improve them?' and 'When will you do this?' Hidden statements in questions nearly always start with a verb, e.g. is, has, will, etc. Check with your intention first, by asking yourself 'What is the statement behind this question?' You may be surprised by the answers you find.

A word about the open question opener, 'why'. When you question assumptions using 'why', e.g. 'Why do you want promotion?', it can feel like an attack and your client may withdraw. Inspection of tfgs need questions using one of the other openers, e.g. 'What is it about the job that attracts you?' For example, when someone says he 'wants to get promotion', the questioning may go something like this:

- What do you need to do to get promotion?
- How can you achieve that?
- What might stop you?
- What could help you?
- Who could help you?
- When will you be able to do this?

Also the follow-up must affirm your client, as there is no point in asking insightful questions and then destructively critiquing the answer. When they reply, 'I want to work more creatively', your reply by saying 'I have never thought of you as creative' is probably not good coaching. Non-verbal responses to answers are notorious here and you may communicate negative views or even contempt through, for example, sighing, a tired smile, raised eyebrow, inflected voice or inappropriate laughter.

Many coaches use the question HDTMYF? or HDYF? instead of empathy. This is the acronym for 'How does that make you feel?' or 'How do you feel?' As effective coaching depends on the relationship which exists between coach and client, you will already be aware of your client's feelings in order to respond with empathy so the question should not be necessary. Either of the two questions invites over-disclosure and you may be faced with feelings you do not feel competent to handle. For example,

> Martin could respond to Peter's resistance by asking 'How do you feel?' Peter may reply, 'Awful, nothing, nothing to live for – like school – my teacher, he took advantage', and Peter dissolves into tears. Martin would now be seriously out of his depth.

Note: This may seem unlikely but in a recent UK study, 13 per cent of respondents reported having been abused as children: this represents 1.5 million individuals in the UK alone.

Multiple questions are really two or more questions in one. For example, if you say to your client, 'What went wrong and what are you going to do about it?' You are asking a multiple question. Multiple questions are confusing as your client will not know which part of the question to answer. They are likely to answer the easy question with 'it was bad weather and we had no customers' rather than the important question about what he can do to attract more customers.

Rhetorical questions are really closed questions. They have to be answered with a 'yes' or 'no'. For example, 'You didn't get the window done in time, did you?' is closed and is also a leading question with a hidden statement. It leads the employee concerned to agree with the statement. Another kind of leading question is 'How hard can it be?' which leads a client either to agree that something is not difficult or feel incompetent.

Surface and deep meanings

As a coach, you will listen carefully to your employee or client. You may find the idea of surface and deep meanings useful in your coaching. These are the meanings in what they are saying on the surface and the deep meanings which are hidden. To understand fully your client's words you can translate them by recovering the deep meanings in what they say. Surface meanings are deep meanings where your client has:

- missed out some information;
- changed the meaning;
- generalized from a particular instance.

Example of missing out information:

> Surface words: It's just not possible ...
> Deep meaning: *I believe* it's just not possible.

Example of changed meaning:

> Surface words: My manager is against me.
> Deep meaning: My manager *doesn't like me and I believe she won't change her attitude to me.*

Example of generalization:

> Surface words: Nobody tells me anything.
> Deep meaning: *My manager has not informed me about the new system.*

It is possible to recover the deep meanings which underlie the surface words being said in most communications by identifying what is missing, changed or generalized. Some examples are given in Table 5.1.

How can you help your client to recover their 'lost' deep meanings without being too intrusive? We recommend the technique of re-statement, as when your client hears what they have just said, they may immediately recognize what is missing, changed or generalized in the words they have used. In most cases the power of re-statement is enough. The use of repetition and re-statement is natural in some languages but less acceptable in English so for coaches working in English the process feels somewhat alien at first and you need to be careful not to parrot. We will give examples of

Table 5.1 Recovering deep meanings from surface meanings

Surface meanings (words used)	How the meaning is altered	Deep meaning
It's just not possible	Missing information	I believe it's not possible
Nobody tells me anything	Generalization	My manager has not informed me about the new rates of pay
Obviously	Missing information	It is obvious to me that…
He never considers my ideas	Generalization	He did not consider my idea on X and Y occasion
He has an attitude problem	Missing information	I am annoyed by some of his X and Y behaviour
They always forget	Generalization	X and Y forgot on W and Z occasions
I must get on	Missing information	I want to be finished by six
No-one ever talks to me	Generalization	My colleagues X and Y didn't talk to me on W and Z occasion
They don't like me	Missing information and changing meaning	I believe that X and Y don't like me and I believe they will not change their attitude to me
He is never here – he is always on courses	Generalization	He was not here on days X and Y when he was away on courses

re-statement later. However, when you recover deep meanings in coaching, you put your client in the same state as Socrates' slave, i.e. he feels a difficulty. Hence you may then choose to formulate your questions in a way that will help your client to realize their deep meanings and we describe how to do this in Table 5.2. Offering empathy first will switch on your client to the information which follows. This gives it a better chance of being heard and understood.

As a coach you can work with your client's deep meanings by gentle questioning without putting them off. We cannot stress too much the importance of already having offered your client some empathy and we include some ideas in the table. When you do offer empathy, your client may well alter their surface words to include their deep meaning as you have created some trust in the relationship. Thereafter it is possible to recover the 'lost' meanings by doing the following:

- calling attention to what is missing in your client's statement;
- analysing a meaning that has been changed;
- questioning a generalization.

Table 5.2 Empathic responses + recovery questions

Surface words	Deep meaning	Empathy and recovery question
It's just not possible	I believe it's just not possible	Gosh that sounds a bit hopeless. What makes it not possible?
My manager is against me	I believe my manager is against me and she won't change her attitude to me	You don't feel good about your manager. How does she seem to be against you?
Nobody tells me anything	My manager has not informed me about the new rates of pay	You feel out of the loop on pay. What is it you want to know exactly?
Obviously	It is obvious to me that …	You seem sure about this. What makes it obvious to you?
He never considers my ideas	He did not consider my idea on X and Y occasion	That is disappointing for you. When did this happen?
She has an attitude problem	I am annoyed because she avoids some jobs like checking stock	I guess you feel annoyed with her because she refuses to check the stock. How can you persuade her to do this?
They always forget	My colleagues forgot to send in orders twice last week	You must feel annoyed by this. Who forgot? When did this happen?
No-one ever talks to me	My colleagues X and Y haven't spoken to me this week	That must feel lonely. Who didn't speak to you? or When did this happen?
They don't like me	I believe that X and Y don't like me	I guess that doesn't feel good. Who do you think doesn't like you? What makes you think that?
He is never here – always away on courses	He was away on a course last week and last month	You feel alone with the job. When were the courses?
People don't understand	It seems to me that X and Y don't understand	That's a pity. Who are people? or What makes you think they don't understand?
The best option is …	The best option compared to X and Y	You feel confident. It's the best option compared to what?

Developmental coaches will use open questions to help clients to generate their own goals, their assumptions and the tfgs in their work and lives. Questioning comes after contributions have been received with re-statement, and empathy without judgement, so that some trust and confidence have been established.

Another type of questioning which can be helpful is what is known as 'Clean Language'.

Clean Language

The idea of 'Clean Language' came from the work of David Grove, a New Zealander who drew on his Maori ancestry, to develop clean coaching. David was an inspirational psychologist, who, while working with trauma victims, found that clients would use metaphor to express their pain.

His questions use the client's metaphors, their own words and added no assumptions. This series of questions, known as 'Clean Language', enables clients to work with their own patterns, issues and changes. The use of 'Clean Language' honours your client and brings into their awareness some of the feelings which they may be keeping hidden. Clean Language is suitable for developmental coaching and it is claimed that transformation follows.

Using Clean Language helps people to convey their own meaning, free of tfgs or other distracting interpretation from others.

Clean Language is:

- questioning
- discussion
- discovering
- exploring
- working with people's own personal metaphors.

What is a metaphor? A metaphor is the use of imagery, to represent thoughts and feelings. Spoken and written language is full of metaphors, for example:

- sick as a dog;
- over the moon;
- soft as putty.

Metaphors and imagery are very useful in coaching because they can wrap complex information, including emotional information, into a relatively small package. (Did you spot the metaphor there?) Clean Language is most commonly used in executive coaching, but its relative simplicity and its unusual approach to metaphor make it useful in a wide range of other contexts.

We use metaphor easily and naturally to communicate complex ideas, and to understand other people's ideas. Metaphor appears in: great speeches (President Obama's inauguration); powerful writing (Shakespeare's 'All the world's a stage'); adverts (car adverts as animals); and everyday speech (I feel like a cat with two tails).

Clean Language uses the casual metaphors that occur naturally in speech to bring unconscious thoughts and feelings into our awareness, where they can be shared and enjoyed – and understood. This significant feature of Clean Language has many practical applications, for example:

- Does your client seem preoccupied with a matter but unable to explain it? Using Clean Language questions can develop that message from your client's subconscious into more detailed thoughts, so turning it into something really useful. For example when Peter (the loss adjuster above) says: 'They don't appreciate me.' Martin's response, 'And what kind of appreciate is appreciate?' Peter answers, 'I'd just like some respect from these youngsters.'
- Clean Language can greatly enhance communication, e.g. people often assume shared understanding but the details of each person's metaphors are unique. Use Clean Language and you'll discover the meanings behind a person's words. For instance, in response to Peter's comment, 'Mine is trashed', Martin says: 'And what kind of trashed is trashed?' Peter answers, 'I feel like rubbish.'
- Clean Language can be used to discover people's motivations at a profound level as metaphors may reveal their values, and drive their behaviour. For instance, Peter's statement, 'the kind of respect which is given to seniors' reveals his concept of seniority.
- Using Clean Language to explore a person's own metaphors creates a bridge between the conscious and unconscious minds. This is a powerful aid towards enhancing rapport and helping people to achieve a desired change. In response to Martin's question, 'Is there anything else about senior?', Peter develops his concept of respect and senior to include his power to support and guide his team. Becoming aware of the metaphors around a difficulty encourages a different kind of thinking, which can lead to transformation.

In developing Clean Language, David Grove devised a set of Clean Questions. 'Clean' in this context meant that the questions introduce as few of your own assumptions and metaphors as possible, giving your client maximum freedom for their expressions. The cleaner the questions are, then the more effectively your client's metaphors can be developed into powerful resources like self-awareness and understanding for their chosen change.

Clean Language principles

The four fundamental principles of Clean Language are:

- Listen attentively and speak slowly.
- Keep your opinions and advice to yourself as far as possible.
- Ask Clean Language questions to explore a person's metaphors (or everyday statements).
- Listen to the answers and then ask more Clean Language questions about what the other person has said.

A client, Peter, the loss adjuster, working on a career issue with his coach. An example of unclean language with their career issues would be:

Client: I don't know what to do.
Coach: What do you want to do?
Client: I don't know that either.

This exchange is trapped in thinking-mode and Clean Language is believed to access the feelings which are revealed so far. Grove suggested three kinds of questions: (1) developing; (2) sequence or source; and (3) intention. The coach's question is always preceded by 'and'. An example of Clean Language, used by Martin, the executive coach, above, with his client, Peter, the loss adjuster, follows.

Developing questions in Clean Language

Client: I don't know what to do.
Coach: And what kind of don't know is don't know?
Client: I'm stuck.
Coach: And is there anything else about don't know?
Client: Well, sort of confused.
Coach: And where is confused?
Client: I'm all mixed up in my head.
Coach: And that's mixed up like what?
Client: Like when I have to choose a friend to invite to tea.
Coach: And what kind of friend is friend?
Client: A good friend.
Coach: And what kind of good is good?
Client: One who is loyal.
Coach: And what kind of loyal is loyal?
Client: Not letting people down.
Coach: And that's like what?
Client: Like me leaving my business partner in the lurch – it feels disloyal.

Sequence and source questions in Clean Language

Coach: And is there a relationship between stuck and loyal?
Client: I get stuck when I can't decide who to invite.

Coach: And when you can't decide, what happens to you?
Client: I feel guilty.
Coach: And then what happens?
Client: I can't bear it.
Coach: And what happens just before you can't bear it?
Client: I have let them down.
Coach: And where could can't bear it have come from?
Client: I don't want to let down my friend.

Intention questions in Clean Language

Client: I want to make up my mind.
Coach: And what would you like to happen?
Client: Me not to let my business partner down.
Coach: And what needs to happen for you not to let your business partner down?
Client: I need to stay on.
Coach: And can staying on happen?

The first two questions: 'What kind of X is that X?' and 'Is there anything else about X?' are the most commonly used. As a general guide, these two questions account for around 50 per cent of the questions asked in a typical Clean Language session.

The process seems peculiar and would sound odd in everyday conversation especially as Grove recommends that the coach should:

- use slower speech time;
- use a deeper voice tonality;
- imitate your client's pronunciation and emphasis (even accent).

Grove's nine basic questions for clean language are:

1. And what kind of ....is that.............?
2. And is there anything else about..........?
3. And where is.........?
4. And whereabouts?
5. And what happens next?
6. And then what happens?
7. And what happens just before..........?
8. And where does/could.........come from?
9. And that's...........like what?

Coaches will immediately grasp the usefulness of this tool for working with their developmental clients, although they will want to adapt it to their own particular circumstances and may not use it in its pure (therapeutic) form. Its main disadvantage is the time it takes to work through the questions, so you need plenty of time for clean coaching.

How questioning helps your client

Enabling questions are different in kind from interrogative questions, but may be equally probing. The main purpose of enabling questioning is for you as coach to enable your client to change. You may also use questions to clarify their situation with them, help them to reflect upon their actions, consider and reconsider their views of reality, and generate their own solutions.

Using re-statement and empathy coupled with open questions will enable your client to look into forgotten aspects of their behaviour, such as their tendency to sulk when feeling unappreciated, a forgotten feeling from childhood. Forgotten material is in your client's Top Secret File so can be accessed. Where your questioning reveals forgotten material, your client may wish to consider how this affects their current responses. Once the forgotten feeling is understood and accepted, there is no need to explore it further.

Byron Katie: Is it true?

This section is based on the method of Byron Katie known as 'The Work' from her book, *Loving What Is* (2002). Modern neuroscience has identified a tendency in the human brain, driven by emotion, to fabricate ideas that do not necessarily accord with the truth. So we tell ourselves stories to suit. She suggests that we challenge our story-telling self and expose it to rigorous questioning.

The process Katie demonstrates begins with putting thoughts on paper by means of a written worksheet. Writing stops the left brain in its tracks before it can outsmart you by telling you a story. Katie presents a worksheet entitled 'Judge your neighbour'. The worksheet is simple and can be found on www.thework.com in the section 'Do the work'. The questions invite judgement and even childish and petty responses are encouraged by the title. The judge-your-neighbour worksheet is confidential.

The work was developed for use in relationship coaching but the questions can be applied to any situation. Their emphasis on relationship makes them relevant for developmental coaching. For instance, the questions adapted are as follows:

- Who angers or disappoints you?
- What is it about them that you didn't or still don't like?
- How do you want them to change?
- What do you want them to do?
- What is it they should or shouldn't do, be, think or feel?

- Do you need anything from them?
- What do they need to do in order for you to be happy?
- What do you think of them? Make a list.
- What is it that you don't ever want to experience with that person, thing or situation again?

The responses are then applied to Katie's four key questions plus turnaround as given below:

1. Is it true?
2. Can you absolutely know that it's true?
3. How do you react when you think that thought?
4. Who would you be without the thought?

And turn it around (i.e. reverse your original statement about the person who angers or disappoints you).

An example of using the Byron Katie method for developmental coaching is given in the case study below:

> My client Tom is managing director of his company in a multinational commodities group. He is based in the UK. His relationship with a fellow director, Jake, who is based in Asia, is troubling him, as Jake seems to take any and every opportunity to put him down. This happens in teleconferences and Skype meetings as well as the rare face-to-face events. Tom has recently uncovered evidence of Jake making decisions without consultation which have affected his business negatively. Tom feels threatened by this and is pretty sure that Jake is out to get him. He is unsure about how to proceed but desperately does not want to rock the boat in such uncertain economic times. On completion of the Katie worksheet, empathic responses to Tom included:
>
> - You felt put down when Jake disputed your figures at the group conference.
> - You must have felt annoyed by Jake taking decisions without consultation.
> - You feel rather threatened by Jake – you are torn between confronting him and ignoring him.

It is important here to stress that just because Tom wants to improve the relationship with Jake doesn't mean that the guy is not gunning for him.

After completing the Katie worksheet, my client identified the main issues as his lack of trust in his colleague and the disappointment with him acting without consulting with him. He identified what Jake was doing and saying which made him feel 'put down', and he also identified what he wanted Jake to do differently particularly in relation to business decisions and consultation.

The 'is it true?' question was particularly useful in establishing how Jake made Tom feel in teleconferences and Skype meetings.

When Tom did the turnaround on this, he knew that he wanted to raise the issue with Jake somehow. He chose a private email to do this and Jake responded with concern about the effect of his thoughtless behaviour. This does not mean that Jake changed immediately or indeed ever did, but Tom had tested his reactions to Jake and was satisfied that they did not have malicious intent. On the issue of consultation, Jake had again acted thoughtlessly and it turned out that other colleagues were concerned about his actions too. The group directors met and agreed a written procedure which included recognition of the need for consultation.

In this case, Jake's motives were revealed as benign but the method can uncover less than perfect motives, if they are there.

Summary

The purpose of questioning in coaching and different types of questioning were explored in this chapter as well as the link with empathy to make questioning more effective. Questioning too soon may put off an employee who is anxious about their performance, and empathy followed by questioning is recommended. The origins of open questioning and Socrates were discussed and readers were invited to ask themselves what the statement is behind their so-called open question. Examples were given of using open questions to recover deep meanings in your client's surface words. Also included were the techniques of Clean Language and the 'Is it true?' method of Byron Katie.

6   Using the NEWW model

In this chapter, we present the NEWW model of coaching. NEWW stands for NOW, EMPATHY, WHAT, WHEN. The model specifically requires the use of empathy by the coach as part of its structure. As far as we are aware, there is no model which specifically requires the use of empathy by the coach. The E in the acronym stands for Empathy to ensure that it is included. However, each of the four stages uses empathy and we illustrate this through coaching stories with analysis of the skills used throughout.

The NEWW model

The model is based on the principles of Carl Rogers' and Gerard Egan's problem-management structure. Rogers' approach to change was supported by his extensive research. In his book, *Freedom to Learn for the 80s* (1983), he made it clear that significant learning for a client rests upon the qualities that exist in the personal *relationship* between coach and client. What are the qualities which a coach will need in this approach?

1. To be real, i.e. a willingness to be present, to live the feelings and thoughts of the moment (and this is the subject of another book).
2. Accepting and respecting your client, i.e. believing that the other person is fundamentally trustworthy and this means living with uncertainty.
3. Empathy for your client – the subject of this book.

When a coach has these qualities, they actually create the conditions for transformational change. In the NEWW model, we present the ability to offer empathy as a skill which can be learnt.

The model is also based on the book *The Skilled Helper*, by Gerard Egan (1990). He built on and developed the principles of Carl Rogers in terms of the skills needed to help clients to learn and change. The model defines the skills needed for a coach to act as a 'skilled helper' to their client. The skill which tends to be invisible in coach training is empathy and this is why it appears in the model as a distinct stage as well as being used in all four stages.

The model begins with the existing situation your client is in, offering empathy as a clear step, then explores alternatives, and finally establishes what is to be done and when. The model explicitly calls for empathy.

This happens in four stages:

1. *NOW* – the current situation for your client and how they are feeling about it. Goals may emerge here but not in stage 2.
2. *EMPATHY* – offer this before questioning to build trust and establish a relationship with your client.
3. *WHAT* – what needs to happen for your client to achieve their goal and how do they feel about that? This is where questioning features strongly.
4. *WHEN* – your client decides on their chosen action – how might they feel about it?

The model can be used in performance coaching, engagement coaching, development coaching and team coaching. We give examples of the model being used in each situation below.

Using NEWW in performance coaching: Jo and Angela

A reminder about performance coaching. The objectives for performance coaching are provided by the company. For a busy manager, NEWW can be used as part of a normal performance management interaction. The departmental manager, Jo, first introduced in Chapter 2, can use the model with one of her supervisors, Angela, as follows:

- *NOW*: Jo establishes the existing situation by first asking the performance question: 'How did we do on sales last week, Angela?' Angela responds with: 'Well, not good I'm afraid, it's a shame it hasn't been achieved again and I think the company needs to revise its plans.' Her voice suggests impatience. Jo, who is new to the role and has tough targets to meet herself, resists the temptation to start asking why the section has missed its target. To give herself time to compose an empathic response, she restates the relevant part of what Angela has said. Jo says: 'The target hasn't been achieved again' and then partial and primary empathy: 'You sound disappointed.' It is partial because she has not empathized with Angela's impatience with the company, revealed in her voice, and it is primary because she has responded to Angela's disappointment expressed in her words and voice and possibly in her posture. Both are in present mode.

- *EMPATHY*: Angela immediately feels able to discuss the reasons for the shortfall, which she thinks might be the weather, and what she did to try to improve the situation by promoting appropriate lines for Valentine's Day. Jo is now at the stage where she ensures that Angela's important feelings have been attended to. She says: 'You put your mind to the issue, and you must have been frustrated that you didn't get a result on this.' Jo has used primary empathy in past mode. Angela is reassured that her boss Jo has totally understood her situation and is now ready to consider the next stage.

- *WHAT*: Jo asks: 'What do you think might help?' and they discuss taking one of Angela's team from checking stock to helping in the fitting rooms, often a major factor in lingerie sales. Although Angela made the suggestion, she looks hesitant and Jo says: 'You're not sure if that will help ...' and Angela says: 'No, I am just concerned about getting the stock out.' Jo says: 'You need to feel confident that the peg panels and gondolas are filled in good time.' After offering primary empathy in present mode, Jo assures Angela that if help is needed to stock the gondolas, she will authorize it.

- *WHEN*: Jo asks Angela when the best time is for this change of responsibility for her team member and Angela says: 'I will probably broach it after the weekend.' Jo immediately detects that 'broach' may mean Angela will feel slightly apprehensive and, on checking with her, 'You sound hesitant ...' discovers that the team member concerned does not like customer contact and prefers to re-stock. Jo offers Angela primary empathy in future mode, saying, 'I guess you might feel hesitant if she is resistant, and I want you to know that I am absolutely behind you in this decision.'

A competent manager can use NEWW as part of their day-to-day work and many are already operating in an empathic way with their staff.

Using NEWW in engagement coaching: James and Anita

James can use the model with Anita, the newest member of his team of junior buyers. Anita does not seem totally enthusiastic about her work and there are doubts about her level of engagement with the company and her role in it.

Anita joined N&T six months ago after gaining her fashion degree. She performed well at the selection centre and was noticed by James as particularly creative in some of the individual tasks. However, she was less competent when required to work in collaboration with others. She has been through the usual orientation sessions in the business, and a series of placements in store to help her to understand the range of roles in retail before she takes up her own role as junior buyer.

James has received coach training and is aware of the level of empathy which is appropriate in engagement coaching. The objectives of the coaching remain those of the company and James uses the model to increase Anita's engagement with her work. He sets up a series of 'catch-up' sessions with each member of his team and this is Anita's session. He will be hoping for commitment and positive attitudes as a result.

- *NOW*: Here James establishes the existing situation for Anita through a combination of listening, re-statement, empathy and summary. At this first stage of the model, James is checking out the facts and feelings in Anita's situation. He invites Anita to talk first by saying, 'Tell me how things are going for you.' She avoids eye contact and says: 'Fine' and he waits. She says: 'Well, actually...' and he waits. She says: 'You know, I'm not sure if this is the job for me – I am not actually designing anything.' James offers partial primary empathy, 'You're feeling unsure.' Anita now looks directly at James and says: 'I was so happy at uni and was hoping for a job in fashion design – this doesn't feel quite right for me.' James responds, 'You were happy at uni, you gained a good degree and you were hoping for a job in fashion design – you say you're not sure the job is for you.' He makes sure that he is aware of and states all the relevant facts as well as acknowledging some of her feelings about her situation.
- *EMPATHY*: James may use a Clean Language question here and ask Anita, 'What kind of not quite right is that?' She responds, 'I absolutely loved our design projects and I am missing that here – I am not designing anything.' James responds with primary empathy, 'You miss doing design – you enjoyed your design projects. Tell me about them.' Anita talks about her very successful design projects which were all carried out with others. She says: 'We shared our work and gave each other great ideas, it was a good time.' James says: 'You were happy because you shared with colleagues and it was productive. How could this happen here?' Anita says that she would like to work more with her colleagues but as she is so new... and the targets they are given are individual rather than joint. James says: 'So you want to work with the others and you feel a bit shy to suggest it. What can I do to help?'
- *WHAT*: Anita says that if James were to include some joint targets within the team objectives, then she would be able to bring ideas to her colleagues more easily. She is sure that as a group of buyers they can influence design particularly where they are working in long-standing vertical relationships with their suppliers. She is sounding a lot more hopeful and looking more interested rather than her avoiding posture at the start of the session. James says: 'This idea interests you and you seem keen to do this.' 'Yes, I am,' she says.

- *WHEN*: James states that he intends to emphasize the existing team targets and stress how individual objectives can be joined up to support them. He suggests the next team briefing a week later for this discussion and says: 'This will be a change for you', and Anita says: 'Yes, it's exciting but I hope the others will go for it.' James says: 'You're not sure about the others.' Anita says: 'No, it's me that will feel a bit strange having beavered away on my own for so long.' James then says: 'It may feel different as you haven't worked this way here yet, but you were used to it at uni, so I am confident that you will make a success of it.'

James employed partial and primary empathy in present mode at the NOW stage. He uses primary empathy in past and present mode in the EMPATHY stage and primary empathy in the WHAT stage. These stages lead to Anita rather than James making a proposal for change. He offers Anita primary empathy in future mode at the WHEN stage and this is important as it will support successful action.

Using NEWW in developmental coaching: Catherine and John

Catherine is the executive coach who has been commissioned for John, one of N&T's general managers. Catherine will use the NEWW model in her coaching with John, employing primary and advanced empathy because John is working to his own objectives, his own personal and professional development.

- *NOW*: Catherine will soon hear the emotional charge in John's description of being stressed by too many responsibilities. She begins by an empathic re-statement of this as 'You seem tired and rather overwhelmed just at present.' This builds trust between them. Providing Catherine can hold off too much questioning, the real issue of delegation may emerge. This would happen eventually without empathy but using empathy speeds up the process dramatically. John says: 'Yes, I am tired and I know this is my own doing – I need to change the way I live and work.'
- *EMPATHY*: John has ownership of his objectives and is ready to work on the changes he wants. Catherine says: 'Tell me about the change you want, John.' He says: 'I want to be less tired, more involved with my family and not worried about the store.' Catherine re-states these objectives and resists questioning John. She simply waits and he says: 'What happens now? Do you tell me what to do?' Catherine explains that (developmental) coaching is not telling him what to do but helping John to work out his own solutions. 'Right,' he says.

- *WHAT*: Here Catherine will work in 'what if…?' mode to elicit how John may feel when he does or does not delegate and what the consequences are of both options. Her empathic responses to his concern are: 'You must feel burdened with all these responsibilities' and 'You feel anxious if you didn't know they were done right.' Primary empathy stimulates the trust needed for more disclosure. Catherine also decided to engage in some disclosure herself about her own management struggles, so that John sees his difficulty as a normal one for managers. Astute questioning about options and preferred ways of working led to further statements from John which included potential emotions, like 'They will make a mess of it, I will be blamed and I will feel awful.' Again Catherine used the primary empathy of 'You feel concerned because your staff may not get it right and you will be blamed, which will make you feel awful.'

Here as a coach Catherine is working with her client to explore alternative scenarios with all their various options and goals. The WHAT stage is where goals are explored, discussed, considered, discarded and adopted. Again all ways of learning should be covered by first tapping into what John wants or desires, then ensuring that John is aware of all the potential options and finally considering a range of actions.

Egan's seven-point goal setting method ensures that all three domains are covered in this stage. The method is given in detail in our book, *Coaching Mentoring and Supervision* (2012).

- *WHEN*: This is the final stage and does not happen until Catherine is satisfied that she has received all the key emotional messages that John wants to express. Her observation of his body language (hand or leg movements) and non-verbal cues (e.g. avoiding eye contact) helped her with this. She offered empathy based on what she could see, e.g. 'You still seem unsure about this.' If she moves too soon to demand action, John may withdraw or just agree without commitment. The questioning here is action-focused and Catherine invites John to speculate about how each action is likely to make him feel, and how the consequences will affect him. In response to 'I need to give X a chance to check the stock file and report back to me', she responds using advanced empathy in future mode, 'You may feel anxious about that' and 'Let's look at how you might feel if he fails/ succeeds.'

This stage of the model deals with the action domain of learning, so this is where John decides firmly on action, actions or non-action. Catherine will also attend to the knowledge and feeling domain by encouraging John to keep in mind a likely outcome as well as the feelings of himself and others about his planned action. The use of empathy at every stage speeds up the process because of the high degree of trust engendered. Many practitioners achieve this trust by attending to their colleague, reinforcing by nodding and remaining silent, giving space for movement towards options and actions. The use of empathy makes this happen much more quickly.

Using NEWW in private developmental coaching: Cleo

- *NOW*: Cleo came to address her career issues. Her story included the usual facts about her education and what she had done so far in her life. I resisted questioning at this early stage, just listening and re-stating what I was hearing. This enabled Cleo to continue her story, confident that she had been heard and understood. A common expression of embarrassment and hesitancy may happen as it did with this client, and this should be recognized by primary empathy like 'You look rather embarrassed about this' or 'You seem hesitant.' Cleo's story included background about her childhood where, like most of us, there were moments of distress, and I responded to these with advanced empathy in past mode, saying 'That must have upset you' and 'You felt lonely then', etc. However, there is no attempt to enquire any further or start a quasi-therapeutic process about the past. It is background but the client needs their past feelings to be understood and accepted. Empathy does this in coaching, builds trust in the relationship and also provides clues about how these past feelings may affect Cleo in the present.

- *EMPATHY*: Before starting to question Cleo about potential options, I stayed with her feelings about her career so far. When she was offered empathy, these feelings turned out to be connected with her role in the family. She experienced powerful feelings of responsibility to be successful in a particular career in order to please her parents, and felt ashamed because this was not her dearest wish. Cleo's feelings were not expressed directly. They were revealed in her choice of language and tone of voice, e.g. 'should', 'ought', ' must', and a tone which fell away rather than rose in her speech. Her feelings were also expressed in the position and orientation of her body. When she was able to express her feelings and have them received, validated and accepted, Cleo was ready to move to the next stage. This may happen in one session or may take several – each client is different. (A useful rule about empathy in coaching is this: when your client mentions the same feeling several times, they are telling you that they have not yet been heard.)

- *WHAT*: When Cleo examined what she wanted from her life, a huge range of options emerged and this stage dealt with the details of what she might want to do, and how she might be able to do it. What is important here is for me as coach to resist the temptation to take Cleo in a direction which sounds like a good idea to me, but to stay with her rather large menu of options for as long as she wished to stay there. Again, this may happen in a couple of sessions but in fact Cleo did most of the work on these various options herself in between our sessions, arriving with a large sheet of paper and her findings. The discussion then danced between her now clear sense of what she wanted, her knowledge of what was available to her, and the likely consequences of each option. An important part of this stage is my reading of her feelings about each and every option, and the empathic mirroring of these back to her, e.g. 'You sound bored with that idea' or 'You lit up when you mentioned doing aid work.'
- *WHEN*: In this stage, the emphasis is almost entirely in the action domain so that Cleo concentrates on her chosen action or actions. Frustratingly for me as a coach, Cleo may choose non-action (at this point in time) and this will test my non-directive credentials. Cleo found the option which inspired her, which was her love of travel and she researched the possible ways of achieving her aim. These included giving up a well-paid job, deciding on a particular course of action, which involved renting out her flat for a year, realizing her savings, and pursuing a risky trip into the unknown. I responded to her obvious enthusiasm by saying, 'You are so excited by the idea of this adventure' and she smiled and looked happier than I had seen her. Cleo also talked about coming back with no money and no job, 'I will have nothing', and I responded, 'You may be stuck for money when you get back.' These empathic responses kept Cleo in touch with her feelings about each likely consequence and her commitment to it.

The feedback from Cleo was overwhelmingly positive and led to further referrals for coaching.

Those coaches who are comfortable in the emotional domain are likely to be successful and generate repeat business. Their ability to work and offer empathy in the emotional domain may be invisible to themselves and especially to their client. This is often the case with female coaches, who are socialized to offer empathy, and do not count their behaviour as a learnt skill. Many male coaches are empathic, having overcome through training, a tendency in their socialization to separateness and distance. Researchers in the field, often using an evidence-based model, typically do not register the emotional domain, and therefore remain unaware of the power of empathy to generate change and stimulate transformation.

Summary

This chapter introduced the NEWW model and gave examples of how the model can be used in performance coaching, engagement coaching and development coaching. The model insists on using empathy explicitly, as the E of the acronym stands for Empathy. Also the model-in-use includes empathy at every stage, in all levels and modes, so that trust is rapidly established and clients move confidently to action.

7   Challenge in coaching

Coaching which does not include challenge is unlikely to be helpful to an employee or client. In fact, delivering effective challenge is a highly skilled operation. Traditionally there are two options to consider: either the *pussyfoot* approach, a coach being so 'nice' that they avoid the issue; or the *sledge-hammer* approach, where the coach is aggressive and wounding, the traditional business approach, exemplified by some business mentors in certain television programmes. In this book, we are proposing the third option, of skilled, supportive and enabling challenge.

For effective challenge, the coach needs three skills: (1) advanced empathy; (2) the courage to confront properly; and (3) a good relationship with the person being challenged. These skills lay the ghost of so-called 'niceness' in a coaching challenge. These three coaching qualities are explained below.

The trouble with conflict

Conflict is inevitable in human interaction. Conflict can be defined as a situation where what you want and what someone else wants differ on a scale from minimum difference to extreme difference. Conflict is experienced as painful and is believed to lead to loss of trust. This is not actually true as healthy conflict builds healthy relationships. Most people receive no training in dealing with conflict and are left with whatever they learned at home. Many people tolerate conflict and can use it productively, but there are also many who dread it and avoid it at all costs, because early experiences of conflict were frightening and painful. If family life is a series of frightening rows between parents, the growing child will store away that fear in their Top Secret File or even their locked trunk if violence or abuse was present. So destructive conflict can be fearful but constructive conflict can be used to build trust, and lead to creative solutions. When conflict is avoided, there seems to be no choice, others are in control and there is a tendency to blame.

Is conflict inevitable?

Conflict will be part of any joint endeavour, unless everyone agrees on everything all of the time, which is most unlikely. Conflict exists in relationships, forcing awareness of difference. Difference is needed for creativity, and if handled well, leads to change and growth.

One estimate suggests that 80 per cent of conflict situations are based on misunderstanding and the other 20 per cent are real in the sense that values are involved. More about values below. What we do know is that something like 25 per cent of a manager's time can be spent in managing conflict unproductively, i.e. ineffectively.

Why should this be? First, managers often avoid conflict through lack of knowledge or understanding about the benefits of difference, and the conflict re-emerges in other ways. Second, managers may not have confidence in dealing with difference because of lack of training and interpersonal skills. Lastly, managers will experience the fear and anxiety most people feel when faced with conflict situations.

The causes of conflict

On inspection, almost all conflict is rooted in difference:

- *Interests* – the difference between what I want and what you want, e.g. I want to leave early for my daughter's birthday party whereas you want to keep your costs down.
- *Understanding* – the difference between what I understand and what you understand, e.g. I understand that the business needs to make a profit or there won't be jobs for any of the staff whereas you don't seem to get it.
- *Values* – the difference between what is important to me and what is important to you, e.g. I see time with my family as more important than work whereas you work all the hours of the day for extra money.
- *Style* – the difference between the way I do things and the way you do things, e.g. I like to tell people what is required and expect them to get the reason for it without more explanation, whereas you want to have a discussion about everything.
- *Opinion* – the difference between what I think and what you think, e.g. I think that managers are posh and workers are honest and are often taken advantage of whereas you think that workers are always trying to slack for the same take-home pay.

Many differences are based on misunderstandings, misperceptions or assumptions and disappear when they are confronted. Often these are caused by lack of proper feedback. Effective feedback is soon and specific. A detailed account of feedback can be found in our book, *Coaching Mentoring and Supervision*, second edition, published in 2012. When giving feedback as part of a challenge, a good idea is to begin with the positive, i.e. the strengths of the person. If you cannot think of any strengths, it's probably too early in the relationship for you to challenge.

The benefit of discovering things about self which only others can see is very well explained by Joseph Luft using the well-known Johari Window in his book, *Group Processes* (1984). As individuals we may miss aspects of ourselves that can only be pointed out by others. This benefit from challenge was pointed out in the eighteenth century by the poet Robert Burns (adapted from the Scots) as follows: 'O, would some power the gift give us, to see ourselves as others see us! It would from many a blunder free us . . . '

So seeing ourselves as others see us may protect us from making blunders. Effective feedback may include an invitation like 'Would you like to hear how it seems from here?'

Before considering how your client will react to your challenge, you might like to consider how you yourself react to conflict.

First, identify a recent work conflict which emerged in your coaching (as either coach or client) as having one of the five causes given above. Then assess your reaction to it.

- *How do you react to conflict?* You will tend to react to conflict in six different ways. You can avoid it altogether, concede, exert what power you have, stand your ground, negotiate or collaborate.
- *Identify which of these reactions are most likely for you.*

How do these reactions to conflict help or hinder in coaching?

1. *Avoiding*: Withdrawing from conflict situations may not make the person or the issue go away. They tend to re-emerge later often in a stronger form, e.g. a manager asking a supervisor to say no to the birthday request above, rather than dealing with it himself. But avoiding may be easier for one party.
2. *Conceding*: Often encouraged by the organizational culture, 'We don't fight here.' Again the conflict won't go away but may appear in another form elsewhere, e.g. other staff members start asking to leave

early for 'birthdays'. Again it may be easier to accommodate than face a conflict.

3. *Power*: Using power may be effective in the short term but creates losers as well as winners and this will affect future relationships negatively, e.g. the manager insists on rigid rules. Using power may be legitimate when a situation is critical, e.g. a spreading fire.

4. *Stand your ground*: Being assertive may not be an easy option but tends to create respect even if the outcome is not what you wanted.

5. *Negotiation or compromise*: Valued in some cultures, but carries drawbacks as both contributions may be seriously diluted by the process and commitment may be compromised. For example, a series of fines for leaving early is agreed and this results in financial penalties, not the best way to motivate the staff. Usually where power is more evenly balanced, this may be a satisfactory outcome.

6. *Collaboration or consensus*: The emphasis here is on getting the best of everyone's contribution to produce a 'both/and' outcome, e.g. a system of turn-taking for exceptional rule changes is agreed.

How you react to conflict can be linked to your beliefs (often described as irrational) but shared by many of us. Here are some of the powerful beliefs that can drive our actions:

I must be loved by everyone.
I must be competent at all times.
I can blame others.
It's catastrophic.
There are external causes.
I am preoccupied.
I avoid.
It's in the past.
I can't face reality.
I prefer inaction/inertia.
Failure is a disaster.
I must never show anger.
I must never show vulnerability.

The evidence for facing up to conflict is not extensive as Western culture is so bad at it and resorts to damaging wars (power) to resolve difference. However, we do know (through debriefing sessions) what happens when teams resist dealing with difference and adopt avoidance or smoothing over. Disasters may occur where voices of difference are silenced and where assumptions are unquestioned, leading to damaging results.

Who challenges and why? As a coach, you may like to consider whether you have earned the right to challenge by checking if you would be open to challenge yourself. What motivates your challenge? Sometimes there are murkier motives than the benefits to your client operating and you may need to be aware of possible contamination along the lines of 'It's for his own good', where discipline is enacted for the benefit of the coach, masquerading as a concern 'for the good of' the client or employee.

Mediation experts suggest that resolution of conflict is carried out in five stages:

1. Understand the issue from both sides.
2. Confront the issue.
3. Define the difficulty.
4. Search for solutions.
5. Agree on a plan.

This sounds simple, nice and logically obvious. Understanding the issue from both sides may eliminate the disagreement or difference. If it doesn't, the skill needed is *advanced empathy*, a tricky skill when either side is angry or upset. The next skill needed is *confrontation*, and for most people this is difficult, especially if the third skill of *relating* is missing. To confront your client, you need to have a good enough relationship to carry a challenge. The use of these three skills: advanced empathy, confronting and relating, is known as strong medicine, so care is needed.

Advanced empathy

We defined advanced empathy earlier and in order to challenge, empathy must include a deep understanding and appreciation of the other. For this to happen, careful listening is the key as well as an ability to remember what has been said or expressed earlier. Advanced empathy is desperately needed because of the modern use of language (in all media and even in official documents). The use of 'I feel that …' as well as other variations described in Chapter 4 makes advanced empathy absolutely necessary or the emotional power of coaching is never utilized. Use of 'I feel that …' confuses feelings (which cannot be refuted) with opinion, fact or belief (which can). The use of 'I feel that …' makes challenge difficult unless the coach can disentangle feeling from fact.

Tom

Tom is the managing director of a company in a multinational group. His coaching was reported in Chapter 5 using the Byron Katie 'Is it true?' worksheet. He was troubled by his colleague, Jake, in Asia whom he thought was putting him down and failing to consult on important business issues. The work led to him identifying Jake as not having a malicious intent and Jake agreeing to a consultation protocol.

Continuing coaching with Tom, his coach, Anne, noticed that he had spoken about Jake in strongly negative terms, and this was still in evidence, with Tom saying: 'I feel that Jake is out to get me' and 'I feel like he is attacking me.' She offered advanced empathy as 'It sounds like you feel threatened by him', and Tom agreed.

Anne began to suspect that there was more to the Jake and Tom relationship than had at first appeared. She had noted Tom's earlier references to Jake as cocky and being full of himself. The relationship was not going well and other colleagues in the group were noticing the bad atmosphere.

Anne decided to share a guess with him, and said, 'You know, Tom, it seems like you really don't like Jake. If you don't mind, I am going to suggest something which you may not like – are you up for it?' When Tom agrees, she says: 'I noticed earlier that you seemed resentful of Jake, his confidence and his charm with women. I am wondering if you might be feeling a bit jealous of him.' After a very long pause, Tom said: 'Maybe I am – I feel that he gets all the attention in the group even when my results are really good.' His coach said: 'No wonder you feel that way – it must seem unfair.' Tom admitted that he tends to feel jealous around other men having had a struggle to shine in the family, as his elder brother was the golden boy and his parents' favourite.

Also, he had liked one of the women in the Asian team and he didn't get a look in when Jake was around. The coaching proceeded on what Tom would need to do to improve the relationship with Jake so that they could work usefully together. Tom decided to approach the woman who interested him separately from business sessions and he rehearsed a way of presenting his results with more impact at international meetings.

The recommended manner of using advanced empathy in challenge needs to be tentative and careful. This allows your client to disagree, as you may be mistaken. The coach here prepared Tom for the challenge, obtained his assent, and offered further advanced empathy before beginning to work on solutions.

The use of empathy uncovers the hidden elements in your clients which limit their ability to learn and change. For instance, some leaders want to be less directive and open to delegation but find themselves unable to let go of their need to be 'in charge'. Others are so anxious to be popular that they are unable to be direct with colleagues and employees. The underlying feelings which can be found in working with clients are fear and anxiety. For example, leaders may fear that if they lose control, they will become helpless and a failure. Others may be anxious to please others because they have learnt that being well-regarded is essential for them to exist.

Assuming your client recognizes their hidden feelings, perhaps fear of failure or being considered stupid, the process of simply articulating these feelings can enable them to confront what is limiting them. For instance, when a client who is afraid to delegate is offered empathy and is free to express their fear, they are likely to be able to put their fear into perspective and tolerate the possibility that their staff may not perform as they would, that their staff may make a mistake, and that this will not bring the world to an end. What follows is a client who dares to risk the failure that he was so afraid of that he was unable to delegate.

Charles

Charles runs a small furniture business in a busy city suburb. He designs and supplies customized furniture to order. Each piece is made to the specifications of the particular client and if the design is not correct, the business experiences a loss until the item can be sold at cost. He is constantly aware that his cash flow may be compromised at any moment and relies on a large overdraft.

Charles has recruited a talented team who create the furniture under his direction and they have become competent and reliable.

His business is expanding very fast and he has created a pattern book for his team with templates for most of the designs he needs. Each order begins with the basic template and then the particular customer requirements are added. However, he is unable to let go of responsibility for every single order and he is overseeing each one. His staff are irritated and resentful, wishing that he would trust them to get on with it. Charles is also wearing himself out as the volume of business needs him to manage the team, not do the work for them.

Charles is beginning to panic when he contacts an executive coach, Frances. Charles tells Frances about his financial vulnerability and she is tempted to get into a discussion on business plans and financial advice. However, as Frances was properly trained, she resists the temptation and stays with how Charles feels about delegating his craft to others. The feelings which emerge are sadness that he is no longer hands on in the business and panic that his team will make a mistake.

Frances says: 'You must be missing making the stuff yourself, especially when it is your own design.' He gulps and nods. Then Frances adds: 'You seem worried about your staff. Tell me about them.' Charles relates how skilled and reliable his staff are and realizes that his fear is not rational but lies probably in past experience. He was taught by his father who was a stern taskmaster and, although this is why Charles is so good at his craft, he is mortally afraid of making a mistake. The situation where one of his team could make a mistake but Charles will carry responsibility makes Charles feel frantic. Frances sees this feeling in his face and says: 'You look terrified by that idea – let's look at what might happen.' When Charles says he will lose money, Frances says: 'You might feel annoyed about that' and when he says: 'How can I face the customer?' she says: 'I guess you might feel ashamed as this is not up to your usual standard.' Charles envisions the negative feelings he may experience and then in a rehearsal Charles accesses his power to offer a customer an explanation, an alternative or a refund.

The coaching supports Charles while he dares to risk his staff making mistakes – of course they hardly make any and he finds that his fears were largely unfounded.

These feelings may seem unlikely on the page but they are hidden in Charles's Top Secret File or even denied in his locked trunk so they are rarely voiced. Hence these feelings are kept out of conscious awareness, as described in Chapter 3, so that he can function in modern life and particularly as managers in large organizations. As a coach you should not underestimate the power of these fears and the courage needed to overcome them. The system serves to protect and defend a self-image which your client wants others to see or has learnt over time is desirable. However, the hidden feelings can be found when empathy is offered to your client in a safe relationship.

It is not possible to remove the feelings of fear and anxiety as these were laid down early in life. However, when your client is offered empathy, their feelings of danger when trying to change can be managed. In effect, coaching with empathy enables your client to do the following;

- face their fear or anxiety;
- revise and accept some of their hidden feelings;
- diminish the power of their hidden Top Secret File feelings;
- enlarge their healthy self-image.

What if your client is denying their deep feelings? We discuss the boundary between coaching and therapy in Chapter 8. As a developmental coach, you will be well aware of this boundary. When you meet it in performance or engagement contexts, we would counsel caution where feelings are denied and refer the client for therapy.

Confrontation

The word denotes 'Put-in-front-of', so that when you confront someone, you take them by surprise. Confrontation inspires fear because of the common experience of confrontation which is destructive rather than helpful. A great deal of time and energy is spent on unresolved conflict, due to people being unable to confront and deal with it productively. Because it is a fearful behaviour, for both coach and client, they either avoid it or do it clumsily. Impending confrontation generates anxiety in the coach so confronting takes nerve to cope with the natural anxiety of causing shock.

Confrontation is often in the 'eye of the beholder'. Anything can seem confrontational if I'm in that mood, and what may appear low key to me can seem outrageous to others. The confronting effect of identifying taken-for-granted assumptions can be perceived as threatening. Hence, as with advanced empathy, you need to confront with care. The recommended manner of confronting is tentative, using words like 'perhaps', 'I guess', 'maybe', etc.

Note: confronting in coaching has nothing to do with the aggressive combative account of confrontation that is sometimes applied to legal, political and industrial disputes in Western society.

Effective confrontation is non-aggressive, non-combative and deeply supportive of the person being confronted. The power of confrontation lies in its 'surprise' element – the fact that what was previously unknown is now known to your client. Because confrontation is necessarily revealing that which was previously unknown, your client will experience shock, even if they are prepared. A simple preamble is a good way of warning your client that a surprise is coming up! If your client can be 'held' and supported in their 'surprise', then they are free to consider how they might use the information. They have a choice, i.e. to act differently or seek further information.

Has there been sufficient listening and understanding to justify the confrontation? Will the relationship support a confrontation at this point in time? Is this even the right time/place? Is the client in a good state to receive a confrontation? These are just some of the points to consider before launching into confrontation.

Types of confrontation

Let's look at the different types of confrontation that coaching might reveal;

- *Information*: calling attention to forgotten or unaware material, e.g. 'Angela, can I just check? Didn't you say you'd have the sales record ready today?'
- *Experiential*: discrepancies between verbal/non-verbal messages; what your client is saying and doing, e.g. 'You seem anxious about that customer complaint; I have reviewed your response and I'm wondering why you are worried.'
  - *distortion* in what someone says, e.g. 'You say that you checked the stock and yet the file says we have size 16s but there are none on the gondola.'
  - *games* (being played unconsciously), e.g. 'I realize that this happened last week and I covered for your mistake and now I'm beginning to wonder what's going on.'
- *Strengths*: pointing out talents, abilities, etc. that are possibly not being used, e.g. 'I got a sense of your commitment at your last appraisal and I am hoping to see more of it.'
- *Weakness*: pointing out what is not happening; always paired with encouragement, e.g. 'Helena, I have noticed your silence, and the

team is missing your contribution here, especially when I know you
could offer such a lot.'

- *Encouragement*: a deliberate pressure to urge the other to act, e.g. 'Is
  there any reason why you can't share your understanding about the
  design competition with your colleagues? I'd like to suggest that you
  share what you've learnt.'

So how is this difficult operation to be carried out?

The style of effective confrontation is assertive and questioning. Confrontation is not always necessarily negative but when it is, advanced empathy
first will enable your client to hear the negative feedback.

The how to of confrontation

Some types of confrontation are given below with some examples:

- *Interrupt and identify the agenda*, e.g. 'John, you are concerned to meet
  your targets. Can I just check if you realized, John, that you said all
  your staff are lazy?'
- *Explain relevance and give space*, e.g. 'John, I know that you feel committed to your staff and value hard work, but I would be concerned if
  every single member of staff is lazy. What do you think?'
- *Open questions, then LAW* (listen and wait), e.g. 'Helena, you seem
  anxious, when will I see your report?'
- *Educational information*, e.g. 'Charlotte, you seem unsure about this
  product. I am getting the impression that you are unaware of the
  product specifications. How can I help you with this?'
- *Correcting*, e.g. 'You seemed hesitant when you spoke about the
  product capability. I would like you to look at that again as what
  you said was incorrect. Can you do that please and review it with
  me?'
- *Disagree*, e.g. 'You seem satisfied with these results, Peter, and I recognize your view. I'm afraid I don't agree with it. I would like you to
  check those figures again.'
- *Moving the discussion* from 'what and why' to 'how and when' and
  from 'then and there' to the 'here and now', e.g. 'You seem determined, James. You are saying what you want to achieve in terms of
  making a new start with your staff and you've told me why. I'd like
  to hear today how you will operate differently and when you think
  that might happen.'
- *Mirroring*, e.g. 'You are saying that you want to complete your report
  by the 15th.'
- *Validate*, e.g. 'Jo, I noticed that your previous appraisal rated your performance as excellent. You must have been pleased by that. I would

like you to reflect on how you achieved that rating so that you can work as effectively in the next six months.'

- *Attend*, e.g. silent attention after someone has spoken can act as a confrontation as the speaker considers her own words in silence.
- *Values*, e.g. 'Tracey, you said you had mixed feelings about our sales of bikinis to 8-year-olds. Can we discuss how this can be communicated to head office?'

For example:

Rosie

Rosie is a journalist with a fashion magazine. She was having difficulties in being taken seriously at work and she thought she was not being given difficult assignments. Her boss, Marcia, was a large, confident and assertive woman, very fashionable herself, and Rosie felt quite tiny, literally and figuratively, beside her. In the coaching sessions, Rose shivered when she spoke about Marcia. Her coach Sarah said, 'You seem frightened of Marcia ... you are shaking.' Rosie said that she did indeed feel afraid as Marcia could decide her future as a journalist.

It turned out that, because of this, Rosie tended to keep her head down so as not to attract attention. However, this meant that she wasn't noticed and, as Marcia controlled all the work assignments, she wasn't getting the work she wanted.

Sarah offered Rosie empathy, 'You must feel frustrated.' Their relationship was good with a lot of trust. When Rosie had shared some of her early disasters at work, Sarah had told Rosie that she herself could feel invisible around very confident and showy people. It would be easy to demonize Marcia and spend time in analyzing her behaviour. Instead Sarah concentrated on what Rosie herself was doing at work.

In the coaching sessions, Sarah noticed that Rosie sat in such a way that she appeared very small, almost childlike, and diminutive. Sarah decided to confront Rosie with what she had noticed. She said: 'I have noticed a couple of things about you which might be relevant here, would you like me to share them with you?' Rosie agreed and Sarah said there were two things she had noticed. One was Rosie's voice, which was high-pitched and rather babyish. This emphasized her childlike appearance and did not make Rosie seem grown-up. Sarah also noted that her name was the diminutive form of Rose and she wondered why Rosie used that at work if she wanted to be taken seriously. The confrontation was quite a revelation to Rosie, who went away and practised her new voice, called herself Rose and soon began to get assignments.

Sarah had established a good challenge relationship with Rosie before embarking on a confrontation. She had offered her advanced empathy so there was understanding of her client. She had herself shared similar feelings in the past and she was confronting for the benefit of Rosie not herself.

You can test whether the conditions are right for confrontation by asking yourself these test questions:

- Is the relationship strong enough?
- Who is this for?
- Have I disclosed some of my own weaknesses?
- Have I offered advanced empathy first?
- How will I respond to a counter-challenge?

You may also find it useful to keep in mind a list of the characteristics of ineffective confrontation, called the Dirty Dozen in confrontation:

1. ordering
2. warning
3. exhorting
4. advising
5. lecturing
6. judging
7. over-praising
8. ridiculing
9. interpreting/diagnosing
10. sympathizing
11. interrogating
12. distracting/withdrawing.

How do people respond to confrontation? Unfortunately not everyone accepts a confrontation and some people may be defensive in their response. We recommend that when this happens, the coach should re-state the defensive response and offer further empathy. There may then follow a painful process of realization which the coach will need to support.

Relating for challenge

For effective challenge the coaching relationship must be resilient. This means that as coach, you are in tune with the client and the relationship is one of trust and honesty on both sides. Where there is a power imbalance, challenge is difficult as an employee is unlikely to trust someone who can hire and fire them. Part of a strong coaching relationship in which to challenge is an established right to challenge. This right is earned by the coach being prepared to be challenged themselves and having honest motivation.

Being prepared to be challenged gives you the right to challenge. This means that you are prepared to share something about yourself which levels the relationship, e.g. 'I am not a patient manager myself and I am aware of a tendency to be impatient.' What you share must be relevant to the current issue, e.g. if your client is confused about sell-by dates, you can share your experience of being confused, even though it is in the past.

Honest motivation means checking out who the challenge is for. Is it for you or your client? Challenge built on relationship is for the benefit of the other. This is important as your challenge may have dramatic results for good or ill.

The state of your client should also be considered, as in, is this the right time? What else may have happened to your client today? Do they look able to receive challenge today? And one challenge at a time, please!

Many challenge failures are caused by trying to challenge without relating. Relating is the ability to discuss with another person what is happening between the two of you in the here and now:

- Effective challenge is invitational – not imposed, as a challenge which is forced is likely to be rejected.
- Effective challenge is intentional – not accidental but planned.
- Is there a challenge relationship already? Am I prepared to be challenged and have I self-challenged?
- How deep is my understanding of the other?
- Test for climate of support.

Climate of support in the environment

There has to be a climate for support in the environment to make a successful challenge. Check for the following:

- Is there trust? Can people take risks here?
- Are people prepared to disclose?
- Is there a climate of respect for difference?
- Is there an open atmosphere where people can make and own mistakes?
- Is there empathy in the environment?
- What is taken-for-granted co-operation or competition?
- Do people value others' strengths?

A useful matrix, given as Figure 7.1 'Mutual dependence of challenge and support', may help to clarify how challenge and support work together. Where there is challenge without support, this leads to no change, and support without challenge also leads to no change (stasis in Figure 7.1). In addition, lack of support causes staff to retreat or block any change, whereas support with a lack of challenge causes staff to continue as before.

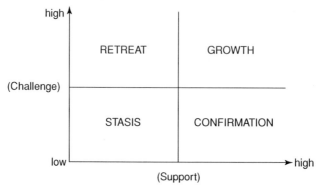

Figure 7.1 Mutual dependence of challenge and support

The essentials in a coach/client relationship for challenge to be effective

What are the essential characteristics that help a coach/client relationship face a challenge successfully?

- *Freedom from role* – a manager is in role for performance coaching but not for developmental coaching; challenging in performance coaching is limited to specific feedback about performance.
- *Spontaneity* – being real and authentic with your client – for their benefit.
- *Ability to remain non-defensive* with a client who is offering you negative feedback about the coaching.
- *Honesty* – being straight with your client about what is happening in the coaching relationship.
- *Openness* – being open to suggestions from your client about the relationship.
- *Being concrete and specific* about your client's behaviour.
- *Attention* to what is currently concerning your client.
- *Empathy.*
- *Being tentative* – recognizing that you could be mistaken.
- *Care and respect* for your client.

We remind readers of the difficult/easy continuum in expression of emotion in Chapter 4. Saying a feeling to a person who is present about the here and now is the most difficult and challenging way of expressing emotion. For example:

> I sense you're feeling resistant, Eddie, I can feel you withdrawing and I feel disappointed.

Relating talk is a complex skill, which asks for self-awareness on the part of the coach, as well as the courage to voice what they are feeling in the moment. It is the strong medicine of challenge and may have powerful effects. The coach needs to be aware of what is happening internally and externally, and make a judgement about what is appropriate to express and what is appropriate 'to park'. Relating talk takes courage, there is no knowing how your client will react, for many, it's a shock but our experience is that when your client recovers from the shock, the honesty of relating talk is incredibly appreciated and the relationship moves on to a new plane. However, it is daunting.

Another example:

> I'm aware that you resent me, Peter, although you haven't said so. I see by your look and your tone of voice that you are angry. I feel confused and I would prefer you to say how you feel out loud.

Really, relating talk is high-level self-disclosure and feedback wrapped together – what-is-happening-to-me-right-now disclosure. This is not personal disclosure but honest expression of the coach's feelings about the coaching relationship and, perhaps, the purpose of the coaching. For further guidance on feedback, refer to our book, *Coaching Mentoring and Supervision* (2012).

When a coach is able to use relating talk in a coaching session, the benefits are measurable.

Rick

Rick owned his own successful business. As a web designer and graphic artist, he had plenty of work but lots of competition. He was trying to understand his own behaviour at work where his team were resisting his advice. His coach, Trevor, a businessman with lots of experience behind him, recognized in Rick a younger version of himself. He established a good relationship with Rick by offering empathy when Rick spoke about his frustration with his team and his disappointment when they didn't get a hoped-for account. Rick sounded off about his people in the coaching sessions and Trevor's empathy helped to calm him down.

When reviewing some of Rick's interactions with his staff, as well as saying 'You must be fed up telling them the same thing over and over again,' Trevor also asked Rick how his team responded to his behaviour. It turned out that they left the company as there are plenty of jobs in web design and they could get another job easily. In the coaching sessions, when Trevor offered empathy to Rick, he ignored it and when Trevor suggested why the feeling might be there, Rick would look at him rather patronizingly and say: 'Well, of course.' Trevor decided to offer Rick feedback about his interpersonal style.

First, he asked Rick if he would like to hear how Trevor was experiencing him and Rick agreed. Trevor said, 'When you say "Well, of course" and look at me that way – it makes me feel rather stupid.' Total silence until Rick said,

'What am I doing?' Trevor described it and Rick became very thoughtful and said, 'You know, I fell out with my neighbour about nothing – maybe I did it to her.'

The coaching moved into working with Rick's style rather than how to sort out his staff. Rick's review and evaluation identified this relating moment as the most important in the coaching. His business continues to thrive.

Summary

In this chapter we have explored the importance of challenge in coaching. Causes and types of conflict were described as well as how people react to conflict. The three skills of challenge were described: advanced empathy; confrontation; and relating. Examples and case studies illustrated the skills in use.

8 The boundary between coaching and therapy

In this chapter we discuss the boundary between coaching and psychological therapy. It is important to be aware of where the boundary lies, as most coaches are anxious not to stray into a therapeutic situation without professional support and training. However, coach training rarely includes the impact of a client's deep emotions on the coach themselves. When this is triggered without awareness, it may result in the coach feeling unable to cope. In this chapter we present guidelines for coaches and draw attention to the value of therapeutic ideas, including the requirement for supervision to support coaching activity.

As we note in Chapter 2, the term coaching is used to describe a wide variety of helping interventions, from performance to development. The key to understanding what is being offered is to identify the objective of the coaching, who owns it, the coaching approach, and the ultimate outcome. Answers to these questions gave us three main categories: performance coaching; engagement coaching; and developmental coaching.

What is counselling, psychotherapy or therapy?

The terms counselling and psychotherapy also describe a variety of approaches. The British Association for Counselling and Psychotherapy give a definition as follows:

> Counselling and psychotherapy are umbrella terms that cover a range of talking therapies. They are delivered by trained practitioners who work with people over a short or long term to help them bring about effective change or enhance their wellbeing.

And, more generally, therapy can be described as a service sought by people in distress or in some degree of confusion who wish to discuss and resolve these.

Or,

> Counselling is a purposeful, private conversation, arising from the intention of one person to reflect on and resolve a problem in living, and the willingness of another person to assist in that endeavour.
>
> (McLeod 1998: 6)

For many clients, counselling is chosen because the term 'psychotherapy' has echoes of the medical model and believed links with mental illness. Another way of differentiating them is to describe counselling as brief and psychotherapy as in-depth and long-term when, in fact, there is a huge overlap. The purpose, process and learning outcome identify the activity, whatever its name, and therefore we will use the term 'therapy' for both. Some people believe that therapy always deals with the past and this is a mistaken idea. There are several therapeutic approaches which operate, like coaching, largely in the present.

As you can see, these definitions are not very different from coaching, but the training for them is different.

The boundary

Performance coaching

Managers who use performance coaching as part of their role are unlikely to come up against the boundary as their purpose is prescribed by the objectives required by the organization. The desired outcome is improved performance rather than personal or professional transformation. In the performance situation, the partial level of empathy is appropriate, focusing on the task-related feelings and leaving personal material alone, as this is not their brief.

However, managers need to be alert to potential boundaries at work.

> For example, when Angela is discussing sales performance with Tracey (mentioned in Chapter 2), Tracey begins to cry. This is happening almost every day, so Angela senses that there is something troubling Tracey, which is about her personal life. She has already altered Tracey's hours to accommodate her need to be with her little girl who is ill. However, when Tracey says: 'If only my husband was still here, I could manage better', and Angela realizes that Tracey's husband has left her for another woman. She says: 'You must feel very let down and I would like you to see a counsellor.'

Engagement coaching

Engagement coaching is likely to engender a stronger relationship using primary empathy but is still working to prescribed objectives, so initially the client's personal goals are unlikely to be part of the process. The client is being asked to align their own objectives with those of the organization. Again, the manager as coach or external coach needs to be aware of potential boundaries:

> For instance, Jo found that one of her team leaders, Debbie, who seemed totally disengaged from her role at N&T, was arriving late for work, leaving the premises for lunch and smelling of peppermint on her return. When Jo asked Debbie about this, she said angrily, 'This is none of your business. What I do outside the store is up to me.' Jo offered Debbie primary empathy saying 'You sound upset and angry,' When Debbie admits to a drink problem, Jo gently suggests therapy, and that the company will pay for it.

Where performance and engagement coaches find themselves straying into therapy, then the contract is failing to achieve the desired outcome and should be revised to include a clear line between the coaching and referral to a therapist. Under normal circumstances, the coach can ensure that they do not stray into therapeutic material by avoiding the question: 'How do you feel?'

For many coaches, this must seem heresy but wait a while. A well trained coach will already be aware of their client's feelings and can choose what level of empathy to offer them. We discussed the impact of the HDTMYF? question in Chapter 5.

Developmental coaching

When advanced empathy is used, as in developmental coaching, the relationship is likely to be more powerful and emotional material becomes part of the process, taking it into potential transformation, and this is where the boundary with therapy is more likely to be encountered by coaches.

When might the coach stray into therapeutic areas? The client may themselves confuse coaching with a deeper need for help and present themselves as a therapeutic client. When this occurs, caution is recommended by the British Association for Counselling and Psychotherapy's head of media Philip Hodson: 'Problems may arise if the distinction between counselling and coaching is lost' (Pointon 2003: 21).

Where does coaching end and therapy begin? The executive coach role (developmental) has been described as psychologically risky, as 'clinical work with leaders shows that a considerable percentage of them have become what they are for negative reasons' (Kets de Vries 1995: 221). This, together with the fearful belief in business circles that 'only sick, weak or crazy people get therapy' (Peltier 2001: xix), makes it tough for executives to admit to visiting a therapist. Hence, executive coaching may become an acceptable form of therapy for isolated leaders with a need for power. How can you as an executive coach deal with this situation? Empathy can help you here.

First, a warning. Helping in the psychological domain can do harm, and, as a professional, you have a duty of care to your clients. An example is the coach who is unaware that their client has a personality disorder and mistakes their borderline behaviour (inappropriate compliments to their coach) for simple admiration. The other extreme in borderline behaviour, suicidal tendencies, may take the coach beyond their competence. The coaching may trigger unpredictable reactions in such a client. For this reason, it is important to become aware of your limitations. Evaluation and training of coaches should identify these and training should include 'how to refer your coaching client for counselling or therapy'. The danger is that the coach believes they are what their client needs and carries on regardless. Regular supervision is a safety net for developmental coaches.

Managers, as part of their role, will use counselling skills for workplace issues which are short-term and appropriate. For example, an employee who has failed a promotion may be upset and their manager is likely to offer them brief support which will include partial empathy. Brief support in this instance is listening, restatement and (partial) empathy which may also be used by therapists.

How can a coach identify the appropriate emotional level for working with clients? The purpose of the work should indicate the level required.

- Performance coaching will normally keep its focus on the organizational purpose, using partial empathy and the NEWW model to structure the process.
- For engagement coaching, expressed feelings are likely to be at a level of intensity that is typical of day-to-day life, such as frustration, satisfaction, annoyance, contentment, resentment and disappointment. Feelings at this level are relevant to the work in hand, and can be affirmed by offering your client primary empathy at that level, keeps the coaching activity within the professional boundary using the NEWW model.
- Developmental coaching may move into areas that are close to the boundary with therapy, and this is why training and supervision are so important. When clients generate their own objectives, they are likely to come with feelings attached.
- Developmental coaches need to be comfortable with deeper feelings, such as hurt, happiness, anger, determination, self-doubt and the intense pleasure that comes from success. They will need advanced empathy in the NEWW model and relating skills to handle where their clients may take them.

Criteria for the appropriate emotional level were proposed more than 30 years ago, and we adapt them here as follows:

- to intervene at a level no deeper than that required to produce enduring solutions to the problems at hand. This fits performance coaching as it stays with the prescribed objective or problem.

- to intervene at a level no deeper than that indicated by the client's expressed feeling. This fits engagement coaching.
- to intervene at a level no deeper than that at which the energy and resources of the client can be committed to transformational change. This takes us into developmental coaching.

(Adapted from Harrison 1978: 555)

These criteria imply that the coach concerned is able to relate to the emotional world of the client. The fear that inhibits coaches from dealing with emotional matters is likely to come from a feeling of incompetence in this area. We would encourage coaches to be bolder in their work with clients, as emotions are the key to their client's learning and development, while at the same time taking note of discomfort in themselves, as that feeling is likely to be a good guide to their competence in the emotional area. *When in doubt, get supervision.*

It is important to be aware of where the boundaries lie, and this is not always clear, particularly in the initial stages of coaching. Hence the importance of developmental coaches having appropriate supervision in order to ensure and maintain safe conditions and boundaries for their clients.

We relate an instance of a colleague working on the boundary in the case study below.

On the boundary

Helene Donnelly, an award-winning expert on forensic paper conservation, is the founder/director of Data and Archive Disaster Control Centre (DADCC). The company specializes in worldwide emergency rescue and restoration of documents damaged by fire, flood and bombing. It also provides disaster management training for organizations wishing to produce or improve their disaster plans.

A seasoned visitor to disaster sites all over the world, Helene offers her clients advice and guidance before, during and after disaster incidents, which has become essential in today's world.

Recently Helene has found herself in a helping role after a high-value residence fire, where she was concerned to find that the insurance company did not always attend to the emotional and physical well-being of the house-owner, Rachel, who tended to be ignored while the insurance company personnel dealt with the value of the contents insured. Rachel makes the point that a support team of insurance specialists, police and fire and security experts all appeared out of the blue but no one was present actually to assist the victim and deal with her post-event state of mind.

Rachel is an international high-profile businesswoman, with a busy schedule, used to dealing with tough business operational situations and, more importantly, clients who expect the very best service.

This particular case followed a horrific fire that destroyed much of Rachel's home and left her pretty traumatized and functioning on automatic pilot.

Then she was advised to speak to Helene who agreed to meet Rachel. From the beginning, Helene made it clear that she did not offer counselling.

In the first one-and-a-half-hour session, Helene allowed Rachel to recall the details of the event and the ensuing weeks, while she noted key points on a flip chart and in a notebook. Helene asked for details of Rachel's behaviour, as it is her experience that people believe they are behaving erratically when, in fact, screaming, fainting and being angry are normal reactions to an event that is not under their control or within their experience. The validation this gave to Rachel was confirmed by her as follows: 'It made me feel that all the emotions that I was experiencing were entirely normal.'

When Helene had summarized what Rachel had been through, she constructed a diagram of Rachel's experience in the aftermath of the incident and, from this, put to Rachel a perceptive question: 'You do not have to answer this question out loud to me, but can you recount what was going on in your life at the time of the incident?' Rachel was more than willing to answer this question. However, this is where Helene explained that she was interested only in the incident and not in some past Freudian episode. Both were able to laugh at this point.

Rachel found the question and discussion that followed soul-searching, intriguing and inspirational. Helene believes that, after a disastrous event that involves the near-destruction of a person's home, there is serious loss of the person's confidence, which can have negative chemical and physical effects. So Helene recommended that Rachel should take high-strength vitamins to support her recovery and do physical training. The vitamins were named and so were the types of exercises recommended.

Rachel told Helene that it was the first time she had been able to talk about the incident without crying, and has nothing but praise for the relationship, saying: 'I needed to talk to someone who understood where I was at that time.'

Helene has struggled to define the nature of this type of relationship, which includes aspects of mentoring and coaching, particularly the use of counselling skills, like listening, restatement, summary and empathy. Helene is clear that she is not counselling – these are ordinary people in extraordinary circumstances. Helene believes a service of this kind is essential in residential or organizational disaster contexts, and she recommends that individuals are debriefed properly during the recovery period. The recovery period may last up to three months. The individuals may also just want to speak on the phone, by e-mail or over coffee.

Most people never experience the loss of a home or their place of work. However, friends, family and loved ones may want to help by saying things like, 'At least you did not lose your life.' These words do not help but only confuse the person more because the person does not understand what is happening to his or her world. Helene recognizes it is not the 'things' people miss but the daily routine and emotional values connected to their homes and workplaces. Once these have gone, they take time to rebuild, and someone has to help with the new building materials for the body and mind.

Here the coaching included working with ordinary feelings triggered by an extraordinary event. The boundary was attended to by Helene's disclaimer, and she ensured that the relationship remained focused on its original purpose and didn't wander into areas of Rachel's life that were not relevant.

What can coaches learn from therapy?

Some writers suggest that coaching owes a debt to the therapeutic profession that is largely unacknowledged. Developmental coaches may be so busy making sure that people understand that they are not therapists that they may fail to realize that they could usefully borrow from this related profession. Many issues which arise in coaching could be better understood by close examination of similar issues in the counselling field. An understanding of the coaching relationship is an ethical requirement for developmental coaches, and their training should reflect this requirement.

On the other hand, the psychologist Steven Berglas has expressed concern in his highly regarded article in the *Harvard Business Review* (2002) about the very real dangers of executive coaching. Berglas notes that the majority of executive coaches (then) came from the business or sport worlds. He suggests that with little or no psychological training, these coaches may do harm. His case study describes a Vice-President with a narcissistic personality disorder which no amount of coaching could alleviate. Berglas claims that the coaching enhanced his grandiosity, leading to more extreme behaviour, distressed staff and damage to the company.

To date, coaching lacks some of the underpinning theory that supports therapists in their work and which enables them to work productively and safely. This book and others (Brockbank and McGill 2006; 2012) are an attempt to remedy this lack. It is likely coaches are operating with their own implicit theory, and they owe it to their clients to articulate it so that clients may choose to accept or reject such coaching. Many coaches borrow theory from the therapeutic world and adapt it very effectively to coaching.

When coaches offer their services to clients, they have a duty to be aware of their own personal issues, some of which may intrude on the coaching relationship with potential damage to their client. When coaches find themselves experiencing strong emotions about a client or the client's behaviour, it is advisable for them to check out the connections within their own life and history, ideally with a supervisor. This is standard practice in therapy, and the process of self-questioning can transfer to coaches within their training, which should include an understanding of boundaries and diversity issues.

Geoffrey Ahern (2001) has stipulated two 'commandments' for executive coaches (presumed as non-directive): first, follow the individual client's agenda; and second, maintain absolute confidentiality from the company. Specific guidelines that emerge from these two commandments include principles that protect a client from breaches of confidentiality as a result of sponsoring and contracting arrangements. In addition, coaches are exhorted to engage in continuing professional development to maintain minimum psychological competence and to take up regular supervision. We would add to these the requirement for professional liability insurance, which the UK's CIPD (Chartered Institute of Personnel and Development) recommends for all coaches (Jarvis 2004).

When to refer your client for therapy

Referral is advisable if your client initially and openly presents with addictive or dependency issues, marital issues, financial issues, family or personal issues. Such clients may be seeking therapy but prefer to say they have an executive coach. You will be able to recognize the need for referral immediately in this situation. The other possibility is that through coaching with empathy your client, while working on their Top Secret File, becomes aware of material in their locked trunk. You may also become aware of signs of mental illness in your client, like depression, which necessitates medication; anxiety attacks where the person is unable to function; alcohol or drug addiction; paranoia; persistent anger or aggression; suicidal ideas; self-destructive impulses like self-harm and extreme dependency when your client is unable to act without being told what to do. Coach training tends not to include mental health markers to help coaches when referral is advisable.

What are the visible signs to look for? If your client does any of the following:

- Breaches the boundaries you have set for the coaching.
- Cries frequently and sobs.
- Constantly asks, 'What shall I do?'
- Has scars on their arms.
- Smells of alcohol or seems 'high'.
- Behaves inappropriately, i.e. touching or flirting.
- Constantly says you are wonderful.
- Says: 'It's hopeless. I can't go on.'
- Says: 'They are going to get me.'

Or your client:

- Has experienced a major life event like bereavement, divorce, death of close relative or child.
- Has experienced trauma or abuse at some point in their life.
- Has low self-esteem based on childhood trauma.
- Shows signs of mental illness, like obsessive-compulsive disorder, panic attacks, self-harming or signs of eating disorders like extreme body shape and shame about it.

- Denies reality, saying, 'I didn't do that.'
- Is addicted to gambling, drugs or alcohol.

For developmental coaching, but not performance or engagement coaching, the coach is likely to uncover ordinary issues about earlier life and the impact of them in the present. However, there is no need to dwell on them. If they persist in emerging in the coaching, then you have nudged up against a boundary and referral is advisable.

Many coaches would find some of the behaviours above disturbing to deal with, and this feeling is a good guide to referral. When coaches feel out of their depth, they probably are. We recommend that performance and engagement coaches address only feelings that have been expressed either verbally or non-verbally by their client. In Chapter 5 we warn against making enquiries about your clients' feelings. Asking clients how they feel invites a move into therapeutic areas. Any self-respecting coach should be aware of how a client is feeling or at least be able to make a guess, as in advanced empathy (see Chapter 4).

How to refer your client for therapy

Many therapists will not accept a referral from anyone other than the client themselves. This principle is breached when a client is 'sent' for counselling and is unlikely to be effective. If coaches *advise* their client to seek therapy, they may be surprised when their client declines or reports that 'it didn't work'. In the therapeutic world the importance of self-referral is well understood and may not be in the business world. For your client to benefit from therapy, you will need to have worked with them and discovered material in their locked trunk through using empathy. Your client may then choose to address their issue in therapy. At this point you may have to accept that your client is protected by confidentiality and neither they nor their therapist is likely to discuss their progress with you.

When coaches wish to refer their clients for therapy, they may like to keep the details of the *British Association for Counselling and Psychotherapy* to hand. This organization holds a data bank of their members and registered practitioners and details of local therapists can be found in their 'Find a Therapist' directory at: http://www.bacp.co.uk/.

Another professional organization which offers a similar service is the *United Kingdom Council for Psychotherapy*, available at: www.ukcp.org.uk.

In addition, clients may choose to seek help from their General Practitioner and this may be the best option. However, clients should be informed about the nature of NHS therapy which is increasingly limited to one approach, very similar to coaching. If your client wishes to explore their locked trunk, one of the other options may be a better choice for them. In any case, we recommend that you simply provide information to your client and leave them to make their own arrangements. Conveying information about a client to another practitioner without their permission undermines the relationship of trust so vital for both effective therapy and coaching.

Supervision

Why should a coach have supervision? A recent supervisee Clare, an internal developmental coach, is described here below.

> ### Clare
>
> Clare is an experienced manager who is a designated coach in a media company Laughing Gas, which produces comedy shows. She is coaching a team leader, Darren (not her direct report), who is new to the business and seems to have no idea at all about how to manage his team. He is an attractive chap and tends to just try and charm his staff to achieve the team objectives. This is resulting in him being perceived as too friendly and he is then unable to discipline poor performance. Clare has feelings towards her client which she believes are affecting their relationship. She brings these feelings to her supervision session with Graham, who provides supervision for the internal coaches at Laughing Gas. Clare reports on her coaching session with barely concealed impatience. Graham, mindful of the three domains of learning, invites Clare to share her feelings of impatience with Darren and perhaps discover the reasons for it. The session will focus on how Clare relates to Darren. The session is likely to arrive at an action which Clare will initiate in her next coaching session.

Supervision sessions will sometimes consider the relationship between the supervisor and supervisee as it impacts on the work being done with the client. The supervisor can interpret what is happening between coach and supervisor and how this impacts on the client.

> Graham and Clare have no difficulty in identifying Clare's impatience with Darren and the reasons for it. Clare has come up the hard way, starting as a tea girl at comedy gigs. The business is volatile and needs to respond rapidly to potential performers to continue to be profitable. She has little patience with Darren's rather precious way of working with his team, calling them darling, trying to be friends with them and taking them to free shows, and then finding it hard to monitor their performance at work. As Clare is speaking, Graham becomes aware of another feeling which he is getting from their interaction. He begins to sense a girlishness in Clare and wonders if she is feeling jealous of Darren's team.
>
> Graham voices this to Clare and she confirms that she does resent the fun that Darren's team are having, as she was never treated so well on her way up. However, she insists quite loudly that she wouldn't fancy an evening out

with Darren. Graham gently observes her change of tone and Clare eventually admits to being attracted to Darren and of course this is affecting her work with him. He has managed to charm her too.

Graham has used the three domains of learning to understand his interaction with Clare. They can now use that insight to work back to what is happening in the coaching sessions. Clare has used the session to understand how she responds to Darren and what to do about it. Supervision places the client foremost as the focus of the supervision session but includes the coach and supervisor as players. The focus for the session is agreed between the coach and supervisor, i.e. feelings, initiating action or thinking.

The level of emotional involvement dictates what supervision is needed for the coach. Performance coaching can be supervised by a suitably skilled senior manager, as part of their performance management, something which should be happening anyway. Engagement coaching will need additional supervision, preferably off-line, something which many companies provide through mentoring. Developmental coaching requires developmental supervision from a properly qualified supervisor, quite separately from the coaching context. As noted in Chapter 2, engagement coaching can evolve into developmental coaching which then requires developmental supervision.

Developmental supervision for coaches is itself developmental, as well as acting in the role of guardianship of professional standards. Thus supervision for coaches is very different from the judgemental and inspectorial type of supervision carried out in business by line managers, proper to that role. Developmental coaching supervision, according to Patterson (2011: 122), does three things:

1. It provides a safe and disciplined creative space for reflective enquiry into all dimensions of a supervisee's work.
2. It is learning through dialogue.
3. It is a relationship.

The relationship of trust mirrors the coaching relationship needed for developmental coaching. As a consequence, the changes are likely to be transformational for the coach. The need to process emotions from their work parallels what happens in developmental coaching. In addition, supervision meets the need for new coaches to learn their trade. Finally, supervision meets the need for reflective practice.

Supervision as reflective practice

Like any other professionals, coaches should reflect on their work in order to meet the high standards required in the industry. The reflective coach is more likely to be professional, if they are continuously checking the standard of their coaching. This can be achieved through self-reflection with learning logs, learning journals, and the like, but the presence of a reflective dialogue offers the best opportunity for coaches to reflect with the potential for transformation. We discuss how reflective dialogue supports reflective learning in our book, *Coaching, Mentoring and Supervision* (Brockbank and McGill 2012).

Supervision offers a reflective dialogue in order to scrutinize and reflect on the activities of the coach while supporting their work. Supervisors who have been trained for other helping professions, like social work, health practitioners and community workers, are likely to have some of the skills needed for coaching supervision. Purchasers of coaching services increasingly demand that coaches must have supervision, just as many coaches find that supervisors offer them much-needed support in what can be an isolating field of work.

Supervision appears as a requirement for coach accreditation with the twin purposes of accountability and development and these purposes are acknowledged in the ethical codes of leading coaching organizations.

The EMCC code of ethics requires that coaches and mentors do the following:

> Maintain a relationship with a suitably-qualified supervisor, who will regularly assess their competence and support their development. The supervisor will be bound by the requirements of confidentiality referred to in this Code. What constitutes a 'suitably-qualified' supervisor is defined in the EMCC's standards document.
>
> (EMCC 2008)

The ICF Code of Ethics for coaches states that:

> Whenever facts and circumstances necessitate, they will promptly seek professional assistance and determine the action to be taken.
>
> (ICF 2008)

The purposes of supervision

What is the purpose of developmental supervision for coaches? The three purposes of developmental supervision are to provide emotional support, quality control and education.

- support for the coach;
- quality: ensuring professional standards;
- providing education or information the coach may need.

These purposes relate to the three domains of learning mentioned in Chapter 1:

- emotion or feeling in self and in relation to others;
- acting or interacting with the world;
- knowing or leading to knowledge.

The purposes and how they relate to the three domains of learning mentioned on p. 13 can be seen in Table 8.1.

Table 8.1   The purpose of supervision

Purpose of supervision	Learning domain
Support	Feelings or emotion
Quality	Doing or behaviour
Education	Knowing or knowledge

In order to cover the three purposes of coach supervision, the supervisor will need to attend to the seven tasks of supervision arising out of the purposes, and these are shown in Table 8.2.

Therefore the tasks for a developmental supervisor include: relating, using counselling skills, monitoring professional/ethical issues, administration and consulting. The first two, namely, relating to the coach and *using counselling skills* fulfils the support purpose by giving emotional support to the coach, as appropriate. These supportive tasks are necessary for the well-being of the coach and the building of a strong relationship of trust for learning. *Monitoring, administration and consulting* address the quality purpose so that supervisors model good organization in terms of boundaries and records. These tasks also ensure that coaches adhere to ethical and professional standards. The last two, namely *teaching and evaluating*, provide for the education purpose in supervision, addressing the needs of coaches for continuous professional development.

Table 8.2   Purpose and tasks of supervision

Purpose	Tasks
Support	Relating counselling, i.e. using counselling skills not therapy
Quality	Monitoring professional standards and ethics Administrating Consulting
Education	Teaching Evaluating

How each of these tasks can be achieved is described in our book *Coaching Mentoring and Supervision* (2012). An example is included here.

An example of supervision

The supervisee is a coach, Margaret, who comes for supervision with Ben, feeling a bit overwhelmed by the issues being presented by her client, Roger.

Roger

Roger sought coaching voluntarily, relating that he is having problems with his boss and may, as a result, lose his job. As he describes the situation, he says that he has lost two jobs in the past because his 'bosses were impossible to get along with'. He states that, because of the increased stress at work, he is having headaches, has been 'drinking more' and is having 'frequent arguments' with his wife. He is frustrated because, from his perspective, she fails to understand the nature of his 'problem', and that she isn't supporting him. The client reports that he is willing to have coaching but doesn't see that he has issues to work on in the sessions.

Before looking at how Margaret might work with her client, Ben invites her to consider and decide on the focus of the session, her feelings, actions or thoughts in relation to Roger. Margaret decides to focus on her feelings about Roger. She has strong negative feelings towards Roger; she is annoyed with him and feels impatient. Ben responds with empathy to Margaret's feelings, e.g. 'You seem annoyed with this client, you sound short and impatient with him.'

The second question assumes Margaret's understanding of the model:

Which of the three domains would you like to focus on in this session?

Margaret says that she experiences feelings of dislike for Roger, and finds herself thinking negatively about him and judging him, as well as wanting to change his behaviours.

So where would you like to focus, the feeling, the judgement or the desire to change Roger?

Margaret says: 'I think what's getting in the way of my work with Roger is my dislike of him. I believe it is keeping me from working effectively with him.'

Ben says: 'So you are concerned that your feelings of dislike for Roger may be getting in the way of your work with him. Are you saying that you would like to focus on your feelings in relation to this client?'

Margaret says: 'Yes, that sounds helpful. There's something about him, about the way he speaks or maybe it's the tone of his voice, that sounds whiney or moaning. He also blames everybody else for his problems. I get annoyed with him and have trouble focusing on what he's saying.'

Ben says: 'Tell me more.'

Thereafter, the session proceeds along the direction which is chosen by Margaret and may include her experience of a friend who moans and blames others.

She says: 'You know, this client reminds me of that friend of mine who was always blaming others and then complaining about the outcome. He really annoyed me and we fell out over it.'

Then Ben might say: 'You are feeling annoyed with Roger who reminds you of a friend you fell out with. That was sad.'

Margaret: Yes, it was a shame.
Ben: What would you like to say to your friend now?
Margaret: Look, stop moaning – we don't need to fall out over this.
Ben: What else?
Margaret: Can we discuss what's getting to you?
Ben: That sounds like you would have liked to uncover the reasons for your friend's moaning.
Margaret: Yes, now I would, but it's too late.
Ben: How is this affecting you with this client?
Margaret: I want to tell him some home truths.
Ben: Like?
Margaret: Grow up. I don't blame your wife for wanting to leave you. She is living with a 6-year-old child. That feels better but of course I can't say that.
Ben: What else might you do with Roger?
Margaret: Well, he's frightened, isn't he, that he's going to lose another job?
Ben: How can you let him know that you understand his fear?
Margaret: That's easy, it's empathy and I know how to do that.
Ben: So what will you say to Roger?
Margaret: You must be afraid of losing your job.

This process continues until there is a shift in the dialogue which is noticed by both Margaret and Ben. Margaret comes to the point where she feels she has choices now about how she perceives Roger. So the dialogue moves into the thinking domain and eventually into the acting domain, where Margaret decides on specific new behaviours she will initiate with Roger.

The supervision focused, by her choice, on Margaret's feelings towards her client which she accurately believed were affecting her work with him. When the origins and depth of her feelings were explored, she was able to put them into perspective and offer her client empathy, as well as then thinking towards how she would act differently towards him.

In summary, in order for supervisor and coach to cover all purposes and tasks in supervision:

The supervisor must do the following:

- be willing to receive and respond to emotional material (support purpose);
- self-disclose where appropriate (support purpose);
- make a firm arrangement for contact, clear records, including a contract stating boundaries and commitment on both parts (quality purpose);
- be willing to share expertise relating to their work (education purpose).

The coach (supervisee) must do the following:

- be willing to receive and respond to emotional material (support purpose);
- self-disclose where appropriate (support purpose);
- agree a firm arrangement for contact, clear records, including a contract stating boundaries and commitment on both parts (quality purpose);
- be willing to share thoughts ideas and opinions which relate to their work (education purpose).

Where can a coach find a suitable supervisor?

Supervisors who have been trained for the helping professions, like social work, health professionals or counsellors are likely to have the skills needed to offer coach supervision. Members of the newly formed BACP Coaching Division are practitioners with training in coaching from a business perspective, as well as therapeutic approaches.

Summary

In this final chapter we have considered the boundary between coaching and therapy. How different types of coaching may lead towards the boundary were discussed as well as how to identify when coaching is near to that boundary. A case study revealed how coaches can work with emotional material without straying into therapy. Options for referral were given and the need for self-referral emphasized as a coaching value. The purposes and rationale for supervision, together with examples of supervision complete the chapter.

Conclusion

This book addresses an anomaly in most publications on coaching – the omission or sheer neglect of the emotional domain in a client. The assumption that questioning, albeit thorough, will address all the needs of the client is a widespread view held in the profession.

Neuroscience supports the need to attend to the feelings of the client through offering them empathy. It is also important to know how this enables the client to work with their feelings and access the power of their emotions.

An overarching view emanating from our work in coaching is the need to find a synthesis between recognizing emotion with that of the rational, thinking side of clients. Omitting one or the other will not enable clients to meet their needs. If one of these needs is omitted at the expense of the other, the client will be left adrift.

Neglecting the emotional needs of the client in favour of questioning is likely to lead to a sense in the coaching of going round in circles. Neglecting incisive questioning and thought is likely to lead to a sense of being stuck and is unlikely to lead to action.

We have also shown how the requirement for empathy depends upon the situation in which the coaching is taking place. Empathy levels depend on the coaching situation from simple performance situations; through engagement; to the advanced empathy so essential for developmental coaching.

Coaching has developed as a process to assist individuals to change, and through them, their organizations. The results to date are not dramatic largely because most coaching has neglected feeling-based learning. When coaches include empathy in their work with clients, the outcomes are likely to be transformational.

Bibliography

Ahern, G. (2001) Individual executive development: regulated, structured and ethical, *Occupational Psychologist*, 44: 3–7.

Ainsworth, M.D.S., Blehar, M.C., Waters, E. and Wall, S. (1978) *Patterns of Attachment: A Psychological Study of the Strange Situation*. Hillsdale, NJ: Lawrence Erlbaum Associates.

Baron-Cohen, S. (2011) *Zero Degrees of Empathy: A New Theory of Human Cruelty*. London: Allen Lane.

Berglas, S. (2002) The very real dangers of executive coaching, *Harvard Business Review*, June, pp. 86–92.

Berne, E. (2010) *Games People Play*. London: Penguin Books.

Brockbank, A. and McGill, I. (1998) *Facilitating Reflective Learning in Higher Education*. Buckingham: Open University Press.

Brockbank, A. and McGill, I. (2006) *Facilitating Reflective Learning Through Mentoring & Coaching*, 1st edn. London: Kongan Page.

Brockbank, A. and McGill, I. (2012) *Facilitating Reflective Learning: Coaching, Mentoring, and Supervision*, 2nd edn. London: Kogan Page.

Burkeman, O. (2012) *The Antidote: Happiness for People Who Can't Stand Positive Thinking*. Edinburgh: Canongate Books.

Chugani, H., Behen, M., Muzik, O., Juhasz C., Nagy F. and Chugani, D. (2001) Local brain functional activity following early deprivation: a study of post-institutionalized Romanian orphans. *Neuroimage*, 14: 1290–1301.

CIPD (2010a) Employee Engagement Factsheet, revised by Kathy Daniels July 2010. Available at: http://www.cipd.co.uk/hr-resources/factsheets/employee-engagement.aspx (accessed May 2012).

CIPD (2010b) *Creating an Engaged Workforce*. Kingston Business School. Available at: http://www.cipd.co.uk/binaries/Creating_engaged_workforce.pdf.

De Board, R. (1997) *Counselling for Toads: A Psychological Adventure*. London: Routledge.

Egan, G. (1977) *You and Me: The Skills of Being an Effective Group Communicator*. Monterey, CA: Brooks/Cole.

Egan, G. (1990) *The Skilled Helper: A Systematic Approach to Effective Helping*, 4th edn. Monterey, CA: Brooks/Cole.

EMCC (2008) *Code of Ethics*. Available at: http://www.emccouncil.org/src/ultimo/models/Download/4.pdf (accessed 18 December 2012).

Gallup (2008) *Employee Engagement*. Available at: http://www.gallup.com/consulting/52/employee-engagement.aspx (accessed 18 December 2012).

Gallup (2010) *Employee Engagement*. Available at: http://www.gallup.com/consulting/52/employee-engagement.aspx (accessed 18 December 2012).

Gallup (2012) *Employee Engagement*. Available at: http://www.gallup.com/consulting/52/employee-engagement.aspx (accessed 18 December 2012).

Gallwey, T. (1974) *The Inner Game of Tennis*. New York: Bantam.

Gallwey, T. (2000) *The Inner Game of Work*. New York: Random House.

Gerhardt, S. (2004) *Why Love Matters*. Hove: Brunner-Routledge.

Goleman, D. (1995) *Emotional Intelligence*. London: Bloomsbury.

Grove, D. (1996) And ... what kind of a man is David Grove? An interview by Penny Tomkins and James Lawley, *Rapport*, 33, August.

Harrison, R. (1978) Choosing the depth of organisational interventions, in W. French, C.Y. Bell and R. Zawacki (eds) *Organisation Development and Transformation*. Boston, MA: McGraw-Hill, pp. 354–64.

Hawkins, P. and Smith, N. (2006) *Coaching, Mentoring and Organisational Consultancy*. Maidenhead: Open University Press.

Hemming, J. (1980) *The Betrayal of Youth: Secondary Education Must Be Changed*. London: Marion Boyars.

Hodson, P. (1984) *MEN: An Investigation into the Emotional Male*. London: BBC.

Hughes, B. (2010) *The Hemlock Cup*. London: Jonathan Cape.

ICF (2008) Code of Ethics. Available at: http://www.coachfederation.org/icfcredentials/ethics/ (accessed October 2011).

Jarvis, J. (2004) *Coaching and Buying Coaching Services*. London: CIPD.

Karpman, S. (2006) *The Karpman Drama Triangle*. Available at: http://www.TA-Tutor.com (accessed 12 November 2006).

Katie, B. (2002) *Loving What Is*. London: Random House.

Kets de Vries, M. (1995) *Life and Death in the Executive Fast Lane*. San Francisco, CA: Jossey-Bass.

Lehrer, J. (2009) *The Decisive Moment: How the Brain Makes up its Mind*. London: Cannongate.

Luft, J. (1984) *Group Processes: An Introduction to Group Dynamics*. Mountain View, CA: Mayfield Publishing.

McGill, I. and Brockbank, A. (2004) *The Action Learning Handbook*. Oxford: Routledge-Falmer.

McLeod, J. (1998) *An Introduction to Counselling*. Buckingham: Open University Press.

Mearns, D. and Thorne, B. (1988) *Person-Centred Counselling in Action*. London: Sage.

Mearns, D. and Thorne, B. (eds) (2000) *Person-centred Therapy Today: New Frontiers in Theory and Practice*. London: Sage.

Miyashiro, M.R. (2011) *The Empathy Factor: Your Competitive Advantage for Personal, Team, and Business Success.* Encinitas, CA: Puddledancer Press.

NICE (2009) *Promoting Mental Wellbeing at Work.* London: National Institute for Health and Clinical Excellence. NICE Public Health Guidance 22.

Patnaik, D. (2009) *Wired to Care: How Companies Prosper When They Create Widespread Empathy.* San Mateo, CA: Jump Associates LLC.

Patterson, E. (2011) Presence in coaching supervision, in J. Passmore (ed.) *Supervision in Coaching: Supervision, Ethics and Continuous Professional Development.* London: Kogan Page.

Peltier, B. (2001) *The Psychology of Executive Coaching.* Hove: Brunner-Routledge.

Peters, T. and Waterman, R. (1982) *In Search of Excellence.* London: Profile Books.

Pointon, C. (2003) A life coach in two days?, *Counselling and Psychotherapy Journal*, 14(10): 20–3.

Reid, B. (1994) The mentor's experience: a personal perspective, in A. Palmer, S. Burns and C. Bulman (eds) *Reflective Practice in Nursing: The Growth of the Professional Practitioner.* Oxford: Blackwell Science.

Robinson, D., Perryman, S. and Hayday, S. (2004) *The Drivers of Employee Engagement.* Brighton: Institute of Employment Studies.

Rogers, C.R. (1951) *Client Centred Therapy.* London: Constable.

Rogers, C.R. (1983) *Freedom to Learn for the 80s.* New York: Merrill.

Rogers, J. (2004) *Coaching Skills: A Handbook.* Buckingham: Open University Press.

Royal Society (2011) Brain Waves Module 2: Neuroscience implications for education and lifelong learning. RS Policy Document 02/11, issued February 2011.

Sharot, T. (2012) *The Optimism Bias: Why We're Wired to Look on the Bright Side.* London: Robinson.

Smail, D. (2001) *The Nature of Unhappiness.* London: Constable.

Thorne, B. (2012) Person-centred therapy. Available at: http://www.elementsuk.com/libraryofarticles/personcentred.pdf (accessed 1 January 2012).

Index

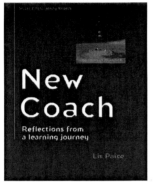

NEW COACH
Reflections from a learning journey

Lis Paice

9780335246885 (Paperback)
January 2013

eBook also available

Coaching is a practical activity that requires no professional qualifications. To the outsider to be easy to do, it can seem easy to do, especially for someone with reasonable life experience and interpersonal skills. However, the skills of coaching do not necessarily come naturally or develop with age, experience or seniority.

Key features:

- Packed with real life case studies and reflections noted shortly after each client interaction
- This is no guru's guide but a real-life traveller's tale - honest, frank, pithy and personal
- Will provide inspiration for anyone on a similar road, indicating the risks, adventures, setbacks and triumphs ahead

www.openup.co.uk

OPEN UNIVERSITY PRESS
McGraw - Hill Education

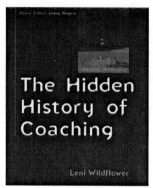

THE HIDDEN HISTORY OF COACHING

Leni Wildflower

9780335245406 (Paperback)
March 2013

eBook also available

This book takes a sidewise look at the knowledge base of coaching. It interweaves the underlying theories of humanistic psychology, cognitive therapy, etc, with the variety of self-help and self-improvement movements that sprang up during the 1960s and 1970s in America, Britain, and around the world.

Key features:

- Intellectually informative
- Each chapter draws links between theory and practice
- Use of real life examples (vignettes)

www.openup.co.uk